PENANG MAKAN

Heritage Street Food Recipes

DAYANA WONG

Published by:

Bulan Press Sdn. Bhd.
2 Beach Street,
10300 George Town,
Penang, Malaysia

www.bulanpress.com

Copyright © 2021 Dayana Wong

2 4 6 8 9 7 5 3

All rights reserved

The moral right of the author has been asserted. This book is sold subject to the condition that it shall not, by way of trade or otherwise, be lent, resold, hired-out or otherwise circulated without the publisher's prior consent in any form of binding or reproduction or cover other than that in which it is published, and without similar condition including in this condition being imposed on the subsequent publisher.

ISBN 978-967-25626-0-3

CIP data is available from the National Library of Malaysia

Editorial and design by Clarity Publishing Sdn. Bhd.
Photography by Hybrid Yang
Printed in Slovenia by Florjančič tisk d.o.o.

CONTENTS

A FEW WORDS
5

INGREDIENTS
11

BASIC RECIPES
19

LITTLE BITES
27

RICE & NOODLES
68

DESSERTS & DRINKS
124

INDEX
150

ABOUT THE AUTHOR
152

I dedicate this book to
my grandfather, who was gone
too soon yet left a legacy
big enough to inspire
generations after him.

Thank you, Wan.

A FEW WORDS

'Food paradise island' - to me this sums up Penang perfectly. I was born and raised on this laidback island and when I left in my late teens to pursue my studies abroad the first thing I missed was the food. The second, was arguing with friends about where to find the best street food in Penang!

After spending most of my adult life in Toronto and London, I am totally convinced that Penang's food and thriving street food scene is incredibly special. Why? Penang is home to so many beautiful cultures and ethnicities that have created a brilliant hotpot of fusion food; Penang's food story is that of the old and the new coming together through the ages.

Street food is at the epicentre of Penang, it's more than sustenance, it's our way of life. To many, street food is everyday food because of the cost and convenience – the search for good food is an intrinsic part of Penangites' daily activities. This can really be seen through the kopitiam or coffeeshop culture; Penang's traditional coffeeshops are not only a place to have your meals but also a gathering spot to catch up with friends or enjoy a quiet moment with a steaming cup of Hainan coffee. Food is so ingrained in our culture that we even use a popular street food dish - rojak - as a social metaphor for our multiracial community.

FOOD, FAMILY, HAPPY MEMORIES
Some of my fondest family memories revolve around food, especially me and my mom cooking for Raya. Whenever we'd cook together during Ramadan, my mom would tell me all her 'dos and don'ts' that her mother passed on to her when they cooked together. Things like, cleaning up as you cook and explaining the types of simple Malay home dishes my grandmother would whip up to feed her family of eight.

I love these stories, especially the one about my great-aunt, Tok Njang, who was a home cook extraordinaire turned caterer. When I was about four or five (when everyone I can remember was still living in kampung-style houses), we used to visit my Tok Njang for afternoon tea when she made her famous (and at the time highly in-demand!) spiral curry puffs. Those were by far the best curry puffs I've ever eaten in my life, period. She had two signature stuffings that were always on order – spicy sardines with canned green peas and black pepper beef with potatoes. My favourite was the sardines. She was ever so generous with whatever she cooked and would always cook extra to give to relatives whenever she had catering orders.

Her sardine stuffing was incredible and to this day I've not been able to find any curry puff to match hers. As a kid, I would sit next to her, and 'help' scoop the stuffing into the buttery dough

> "Penang's food story is that of the old and the new coming together through the ages."

and pass it to her so she could delicately pinch the puffs together. And when I said 'help', I mean picking out big chunks of sardines and stuffing my face! It was usually a ratio of one part into the puff dough, two parts into my mouth. You would think she would be very angry seeing this gobbling monster eating up her wares, but she never was, in fact she would always tell me, 'Eat more, there's plenty where that came from.' This food memory always makes me smile and long for the simpler past.

As I got older I treasured the increasingly rare occasions when I got to sit and watch the heroines of my mother's culinary tales in action. Whenever my maternal aunt, Mak Su Mega returned to Penang to cook our annual Raya feast, as the youngest I would be tasked with peeling kilos of onions, chopping ingredients and being the sentry stirring the ever time-consuming beef rendang by the hot coal burner. I think this is the best way to learn!

My food and family memories aren't only confined to special festive occasions. When I was growing up, it was a normal routine for my parents to 'tapao' street food for me when they came to pick me up from my tuition classes (back then we didn't call it street food, it was simply – food!). I must confess that the thought of eating wantan mee or oh chien for dinner made me work through the math problems quicker! Studying for school exams also called for numerous Ramly burger or char kuay teow late night snacks. Asian parents definitely express their love for their kids through food, although it's not always good for keeping off the extra kgs.

LEARNING TO COOK
The first faintest memory I have of cooking is when I was living with my maternal grandmother. Lunchtime was when we had our main meal, and she and her helper would whip up a big storm in the kitchen from morning until noon preparing elaborate dishes. I remember cutting my finger on a blunt knife trying to help her slice some onions and being a fussy eater. As the kitchen during lunch prep was granny's kingdom, dinner time was my time to explore and cook the kiddy meals that I wanted to eat.

> "Although I cowered in terror when it was time for sewing classes, cooking lessons were something else. Those were some of the best times, learning to cook chicken curry from scratch and rolling little green dough balls to make onde-onde."

When I say cooking I don't mean making nasi lemak or souffles, I started simple by heating soups, pan frying fish fingers and making crispy chips from hand-shredded surimi. This was what 'good' food meant when I was a kid! I still have my first cookbook – *Good Food for Kids* by Rohani Jelani and Angie Ng from 1994 – proudly displayed on my bookshelf. As I was such a fussy eater, I remember my mom making Bolognese sauce which she had secretly amped up with vegetables. To this day, I still make my Bolognese sauce her way with extra mushrooms, carrots, French beans and baby corn, and store this in the freezer for emergency meals.

In high school in Penang, I attended an all-girls school where we were forced to take up home economics. Although I cowered in terror when it was time for sewing classes, cooking lessons were something else. Those were some of the best times, learning to cook chicken curry from scratch and rolling little green dough balls to make onde-onde.

"This book is a blast from the past, a reminder for the present and a gift for the future."

Naturally, I was also heavily influenced by cooking superstars, including Nigella Lawson, Jamie Oliver (I was particularly impressed with his knife skills), Anthony Bourdain and Chef Wan. They helped shape the way I looked at cooking; it was something exciting, fun, sexy and everyone could do it at home! I would get so excited after watching a Nigella episode that I'd immediately recreate her pasta recipe after watching it.

PENANG MAKAN – KEEPING IT REAL

Many of the recipes I've compiled in this book are mostly from my mother (her recipes were passed to her from my grandmother and I assume from her mother and so on) with a fair amount of trial and error on my part to get these down on paper. I say 'trial and error' as a lot of Malaysian cooking requires a sense of 'agak-agak' or estimation. Many Malaysian home cooks would have learnt their skills from a close relative and over the years perfected and modified these recipes to suit their own tastes; eyeballing and instinct go a long way to perfecting a recipe (although I'll be the first to admit that this instinct of mine can sometimes lead me astray, but also to great feats!).

I wanted to compile as many of my favourite Penang street food recipes as possible while promoting traditional ingredients and cooking methods. I know that many younger cooks want easier recipes and 'short cuts' because of their hectic schedules, but to me, this thinking will eventually lead to the disappearance of more and more of our traditional cooking.

Food is not just fuel for the body, it is our cultural identity and encapsulates our fondest memories – the memories of my life, the feeling of nostalgia and the lives of others before me are somehow all connected through food. There are times when I return to the memory of eating a hot bowl of Penang laksa lovingly made by my great-aunt or the ban chang kuih that my aunty used to buy from a seller near my grandparents' house. These cravings can't be easily appeased with a pancake mix from a box. It just isn't the same!

It was during my summer breaks from university when I would plan and make long lists of street food and hawker centres to visit while I was home. My close friends and I would hit the streets and tackle at least 5-7 dishes a day. It was a lot of fun and helped me to discover new hotspots frequented by locals-in-the-know.

My recipes are halal take on Penang street food which is predominantly non-halal. I've covered most of the OG Penang favourites and added in some new favourites such as lok-lok and the

> "I know that many younger cooks want easier recipes and 'short cuts' because of their hectic schedules, but to me, this thinking will eventually lead to the disappearance of more and more of our traditional cooking."

iconic Ramly burger. The recipes are as close as possible to the original recipes. Some ingredients might be difficult to source from outside of Penang but wherever possible I have suggested alternatives.

I would like to emphasise that the way I wrote the recipes was to allow the reader some leeway to explore their own preferences. The measurements are merely guidelines for serving portions and cooks are encouraged to adjust the amount of chilli and seasonings to suit their own tastes. One street food that time and time again seems to be a real favourite of many of my friends is assam laksa. This is a real hit even for those that usually shun spice (like my weakling boyfriend! Ha!).

Penang Makan is my way of passing on and sharing the heritage of my culture as well as cooking tips and knowledge from those that came before me to the next generation. This book is a blast from the past, a reminder for the present and a gift for the future. If you've picked up this book out of curiosity or a craving for a taste of nostalgia, thank you and I hope you will enjoy trying out these recipes.

P.S. Malaysian home cooking is not an exact science and it's rare to have exact measurements passed down from one cook to another. Instead, we use our instinct and personal preferences, or 'agak-agak'. Essentially, Malaysian cooking is about using your gut instinct and personal preferences to flavour your food, which to me is what makes our cuisine so approachable and fun.

INGREDIENTS

Penang state (which includes the famous island, the strip of land on the Malaysian peninsular and tiny surrounding islands such as Pulau Aman) produces many specialty ingredients which help to make Penang delicacies not only flavoursome but also unique.

Here is a list of some of the ingredients that you will encounter in this book, some are unique to Penang, while others are well known and are used all over Southeast Asia. In keeping true to the purpose of this book, to compile and preserve Penang's heritage recipes, I've included locally produced ingredients (which may be hard to find if you are not on the island) and I've tried to provide alternatives where possible without compromising the authentic taste of the dishes.

The best thing to do would be to visit your local Asian grocery store or farmers' market and browse to see if any of these ingredients are available.

---

1. **HALIA (GINGER)**
   A sister fibrous root to the galangal, which gives food and beverages a spicy and warm taste. Ginger can be blitzed into a paste for curries, cut into strips in stir fries, roughly sliced and added to stews, soups and teas for a warm infusion. Just bear in mind that old ginger has more heat than young ginger.

2. **BUNGA KANTAN (TORCH GINGER FLOWER)**
   Torch ginger flower or bunga kantan, is an aromatic herb. The fibrous flower is usually sliced thinly as a garnish or you can eat its soft insides like an artichoke, once it has been steamed or boiled. Its fresh fragrant smell gives dishes a fresh and citrusy flavour. There is no substitute for this pink flower herb so if you can't find any simply omit them from your cooking.

3. **LIMAU KASTURI (CALAMANSI LIME)**
   Calamansi lime is widely found throughout Southeast Asia and is much smaller, sweeter and less acidic than the regular limes found in western supermarkets. The juice of calamansi limes is not only used in cooking but also in making juices. It can be substituted by using regular lime and adding a little sugar or your preferred sweetener. The key to using lime juice in cooking is to add it just before serving when you've turned off the heat, this is to avoid the juice turning bitter with excessive heat (ever tried making honey lemon tea by immediately pouring boiling water into the lemon juice? It will be bitter).

4. **TAMARIND**
   Tamarind is a fruit used to add acidity and sourness to food. Usually sold as a whole or in pulp form (to be mashed with a little warm water before use). Nowadays you can get hold of ready-to-use tamarind concentrate in jars (be mindful that the sourness may differ according to the form).

5. **DAUN PANDAN (PANDAN LEAVES)**
   This is an inedible leaf with an amazing fragrance that is mostly used in desserts and as a bouquet garni in soups and stews. If you can get hold of pandan leaves, you can prolong their lifespan by storing them in the freezer. Be sure to dry them completely before freezing.

6. **DAUN KUCHAI (CHINESE CHIVES)**
   Similar to regular chives but with a delicate hint of garlic. Usually used in Chinese cooking as a garnish or as a vegetable dish in its own right. Chinese chives can be substituted with regular old spring onions but these lack that extra special garlicky taste. Chinese chives feature in char kuay teow and cucur udang.

7. **ASSAM KEPING/ASSAM GELUGOR (DRIED TAMARIND SLICES)**
   Assam gelugor is made from drying assam fruit slices - these add more sourness to a dish. Assam gelugor is mostly used in Malay and Nyonya cooking. You can use assam keping instead of tamarind paste or both, you just have to adjust the quantity accordingly so that your dish isn't too sour. Assam gelugor may be harder to find outside Malaysia so you may want to use tamarind paste as a substitute.

8. **KUNYIT (TURMERIC)**
   Turmeric is a rhizome that stains any food (and even your fingers!) yellow. It has an earthy smell and taste and is usually used in spice mixes or in marinades. You can either use it fresh or in dried powder form in your cooking. To use it fresh, scrape the skin off with a spoon just as you would do with ginger. If you don't want yellow stains on your manicured fingers opt to wear gloves when handling these little rhizomes.

9. **BUAH KERAS (CANDLENUT)**
   Similar to the macadamia nut in texture but mildly poisonous if eaten raw. These go rancid quickly so it's advisable to buy them in small quantities and not store these for too long. In Malaysian cooking, candlenuts are usually used as a thickener in curries and stews. The nuts are washed then blitzed to a smooth paste in a food processor and cooked thoroughly in oil.

10. LENGKUAS (GALANGAL)
Lengkuas or galangal is a fibrous root much like ginger. Although both have different flavours - ginger gives you a special wasabi-like heat, whereas galangal is more minty and fresh.

11. DAUN KESOM/LAKSA (LAKSA LEAVES/VIETNAMESE CORIANDER)
Laksa leaves are used in laksas, Malay stews and soup dishes. It has an aromatic fragrance and is edible; this can be easily added to salads or used as garnish.

12. BANANA LEAF
Banana leaf is typically used to wrap food for cooking much like aluminium foil or baking paper. It is also used to serve food on and for decoration with a purpose - the leaf imparts a subtle aroma and flavour when it comes into contact with the heat from hot food. This is why many hawkers serve their char kuay teow, nasi lemak, oh chien and char kuay kak on banana leaf.

13. CILI MERAH (FRESH RED CHILLIES)
The spice level of the chilli varies according to the variety. Fresh red chillies can also be used as garnish, just be careful when deseeding these and do not touch the white membrane with your bare hands as that's the part of the chilli that stings. Either wear gloves or wash your hands immediately before touching anything else!

14. DRIED LONGAN
A dried version which preserves the longevity of the fruit. Usually used in Chinese cooking such as soups and desserts.

15. KACANG PANJANG (LONG GREEN BEAN)
These look similar to their brother - the French bean – but are much longer (panjang means long in Malay). These beans are more commonly used in Southeast Asian cooking than French beans (which are also available in the region).

16. SAGO PEARLS
A starchy grain harvested from the piths of sago palm trees. When cooked, the grains soften and become sticky. This is usually used in dessert recipes throughout Southeast Asia.

17. GDL POWDER
A coagulating agent for milk which is easily found in baking shops.

18. **HAE KO (BLACK PRAWN PASTE)**
Hae ko, also known as otak udang is a thick gooey paste made out of caramelised prawn stock and is a uniquely Penang product. The process of making this gooey paste begins with boiling down prawn heads and shells into a stock with some added salt. The prawn stock is then caramelised with sugar which gives it a dark colour. Flour is then added to give it its gooey texture.

This is used in many famous Penang delicacies such as rojak, chee cheong fun, sotong kangkung and Penang laksa. It looks a lot like the British Marmite but has a pungent smell from the prawn stock with a caramelly umami flavour. As the paste is very thick and sticky, it is diluted with a little warm water before cooking.

19. **GULA MELAKA (PALM SUGAR)**
Before there was white refined sugar, there was palm sugar. One of Malaysia's biggest exports is palm oil and palm sugar is extracted from the sap of the palm tree. Strangely enough, gula Melaka gives food an umami like sweetness much like its western counterpart muscovado sugar. Palm sugar comes in a solid cylinder-shaped rock or a disc wrapped with dried coconut leaf. You melt it with a little water in a pot over a medium heat but for measurement purposes you first must shave the sugar into a fine dust. If gula Melaka is hard to come by, regular brown sugar works as well.

20. **BELACAN (PRAWN PASTE)**
Belacan is made of little prawns or shrimps, dried under the sun for days and then fermented. It has a strong and pungent smell and when toasted it releases an aromatic smell of the sea. It is used to bring out the umami taste of a dish and is very widely used in Malay cuisine and Nyonya Peranakan dishes. Some cooks use belacan in everything they cook, you could say it's our natural MSG.

21. **CUTTLEFISH**
Brown cuttlefish are large squid with a harder, crunchy texture when cooked. The best way to eat these are to soften them by boiling and using it as garnish in curry mee or as a main component in sotong kangkong (see page 60).

22. **FRIED PUFF TOFU**
Little tofu squares deep-fried and filled with air pockets. Best for soaking up curry and sauces; this is used in curry mee (see page 76).

23. **BLOOD COCKLES**
From the clam family, blood cockles have more haemoglobin in them or in other words are full of blood! Sweeter and more delicate, blood cockles are almost impossible to find these days with their natural habitat of shallow muddy waters being destroyed by modern development. If you can find some, savour these, as they add sweetness when cooked in char kuay teow or added as a garnish to your curry mee.

24. **KERISIK (FRIED GRATED COCONUT PASTE)**
Kerisik is grated coconut that's been fried and caramelised for a long time to achieve the sweetness and crispiness that gives body to gravies, curries and thick stews. The shelf life for kerisik can be long even without preservatives, the reason for this is the frying process (similar to how serunding - a spicy meat floss much loved in Malay cuisine – is prepared). Kerisik is also available in supermarkets in small individual packets.

25. **FISH CAKES & FISH BALLS**
Made of deboned fish meat mixed with flour into various shapes and textures. Fish cakes are usually pre-fried, whereas fish balls are pre-boiled. Both are used extensively in Chinese street food including curry mee and kuay teow th'ng, and even Mamak street food such as pasembur (see page 50).

26. **DRIED BEANCURD SKIN**
Soybean products are widely available and loved by many in Penang. The humble soybean can be made into many different products, from soymilk and tofu to soybean paste. The variety of soybean used determines the quality of the soy products underlined by the big consumer movement for non-GMO soybeans and products.

Dried beancurd skin is made of soymilk thinly spread onto a flat tin and steamed until it coagulates into sheets. The sheets are then very gently hung out to dry. If you cannot find dried beancurd skin, you could use spring roll skins as a substitute (these aren't as delicate and will not give you that melt-in-your-mouth taste).

27. **UDANG KERING (DRIED SHRIMP)**
Shrimps that have been sun-dried which may or may not have been salted during the drying process (check the label). This is nature's MSG and lends an umami taste to dishes. Simply indispensable for Malaysian cooking!

28. **YAM/TARO**
    Taro, also known locally as yam is a lush potato-like root vegetable used in sweet as well as savoury dishes. The flesh has a lovely marbling of purple against white when cooked and when mashed will take on a purplish grey hue.

29. **CHINESE FERMENTED RED BEANCURD**
    Tiny beancurd sold in little jars. Salty and red in colour and usually used as a flavouring ingredient and a natural food dye.

30. **TAUCHU PASTE (PRESERVED SOYBEAN PASTE)**
    A very salty ingredient usually used in Chinese stir fries to add a hint of umami to a dish. Easily available from Asian grocery stores.

31. **ALKALINE WATER (KANSUI WATER)**
    This is an alkaline solution that is used to regulate acidity in baking particularly when making dough. Kansui water usually contains potassium carbonate and/or sodium bicarbonate (baking soda). This is usually used in making the famous traditional Chinese mooncake skin and gives it the dark golden colour. If you are not able to find this alkaline solution, a homemade solution is to mix a little baked baking soda with water. Bake the baking soda by spreading baking soda on a tray and baking it in an oven for one hour. Keep the baked baking soda in an airtight container. Try to avoid touching this stronger alkaline powder with your hands especially if you have sensitive skin.

32. **KICAP LEMAK MANIS (SWEET DARK SOY SAUCE)**
    A salty soy sauce that is also sweet and milky at the same time. The consistency is slightly thicker than normal soy sauce and is used in cooking to add sweetness, creaminess and dark colouring to food. Umami in a bottle.

33. **TEPUNG BERAS PULUT (GLUTINOUS RICE FLOUR)**
    Not to be confused with rice flour, glutinous rice flour has a chewier texture when cooked. Most kuih (sweet snacks) uses glutinous rice flour to achieve that sticky chewy texture. Don't be deceived by its name, glutinous rice flour is actually gluten-free and you can also use glutinous rice flour as a thickening agent in the place of corn flour. If you can't get hold of glutinous rice flour, tapioca flour or corn flour is an 'okay' substitute but the texture and end result may not be the best.

BASIC RECIPES

SAMBAL TUMIS (FRIED CHILLI PASTE)

Sambal tumis or fried chilli paste (see page 25) forms the base of most Malaysian food. You can adapt the recipe to your personal heat-level tolerance. Malaysians use sambal the way the French use their butter - practically in every dish. We use it as a salad dressing, stir fry sauce, curry base, and even eat it on its own. In making this a multipurpose and flavourful paste, I cannot overstress the use of two types of chillies - dried and fresh. My version of fried sambal has a strong Malay influence as this was originally a Malay condiment. We start with the basis of all sambal tumis, the chilli paste.

CHILLI PASTE
10 dried chillies soaked, deseeded to remove heat
10 fresh red chillies

To make the sambal tumis, more ingredients will be added to the chilli paste.
20 shallots or 4 red onions
5 garlic cloves
2 thumb-sized belacan (dried shrimp paste)
3-5 tablespoons cooking oil
2 teaspoons tamarind pulp mixed with 100ml water
Gula Melaka or brown sugar to taste (white sugar is fine as well - but gula Melaka or brown sugar will give your sambal a richer taste and colour)
Salt to taste

In a food processor, pulse all ingredients for the chilli paste with a little water to loosen the paste. Keep in an airtight jar for up to two weeks.

Toast the dried shrimp paste in a pan. Once lightly toasted and wafting of fish, take it off the heat. Crumble it to pieces and along with the shallots, garlic and chilli paste blend into a paste in a blender.

Heat the oil in a wok and fry the blended ingredients. Simmer it for 10-15 minutes before adding a little water mixed with tamarind pulp. Remember to strain the pulp and only use the water. Sauté for about 15-20 minutes until the sambal has thickened and the oil has separated. Season with salt and Gula Melaka to taste. Continue to fry the sambal for another 20 minutes or so until it is fragrant and the colour is a deep burgundy.

Keep this in an air tight container for up to 2 weeks in the fridge and use it as a base for any recipe you like - stir fries, soups, fried rice, fried noodles, soup noodles, anything!

COOK'S NOTE
I like to use dried chillies when I'm cooking. If I'm making dips such as sambal belacan or garlic chilli sauce, then fresh chillies are the best!

SAMBAL BELACAN (FRESH CHILLI DIP)

Sambal belacan is usually eaten as a condiment with raw vegetables and is a staple accompaniment for many Malay and Nyonya dishes.

5 fresh red chillies (deseed if you want less spice and heat)
1 green chilli (I add this to my sambal for extra colour. You can always use bird's eye chillies if you really love a spicy sambal!)
1 thumb-sized belacan
Juice of 3-5 calamansi limes
Sugar to taste

Toast the belacan in a pan until fragrant. Remove it from heat and set aside. Pound the fresh chillies in a mortar and pestle (or food processor) until fine. Crumble the belacan into the mix and continue to pound or blitz. Squeeze in the lime juice, add sugar to taste and mix with a spoon.

CHILLI SAUCE

There's nothing better than homemade chilli sauce made to your spice level.

15 dried red chillies, deseeded and soaked in hot water for 15 minutes
3 garlic cloves
½ cup brown sugar
100ml vinegar
250ml water
2 tablespoons cornflour mixed with 200ml water
Salt to taste
2 tablespoons cooking oil

Blitz the chillies and garlic into a paste. Fry the chilli paste in a hot pan with oil. Add sugar, vinegar, water and salt to taste. Fry for 10 – 15 minutes. Add the cornflour and water mixture. Once the sauce is thickened to the consistency you prefer, turn off the heat. Set aside to cool and store in an airtight container.

GARLIC CHILLI SAUCE

Garlic chilli sauce is used as dipping sauce with all kinds of food including chicken rice (page 118) or kuay teow th'ng (page 96). Everyone has their own version of the recipe. I like mine a little more garlicky and sour.

10 fresh red chillies
5 garlic cloves
1 tablespoon fish sauce (optional)
Juice of 2 calamansi limes
1 tablespoon white vinegar
Salt & sugar to taste

In a food processor, pulse the chillies and garlic. Add the rest of the ingredients and season with salt and sugar to taste. Add water to loosen the sauce. This sauce is good to be kept in the fridge for up to a week.

Sambal belacan

Pink pickled onions

Pickled green chillies

GARLIC PASTE

20 garlic cloves
3-5 tablespoons of water

In a food processor, blitz garlic with water. Keep in an airtight jar in the fridge for up to 2 weeks.

PINK PICKLED ONIONS

2 large red onions (thinly sliced) or 10 shallots
5 tablespoons white vinegar
Salt & sugar to taste

Mix vinegar with sugar and salt in a bowl. Add the sliced onions. Marinate for at least 10 – 15 minutes or longer. Store in an airtight jar in the fridge for up to 1 week. Serve with murtabak (see page 42) or with curry puffs and samosas.

PICKLED GREEN CHILLIES

5 fresh green chillies, sliced and deseeded for less heat
3-5 tablespoons light soy sauce
3 tablespoons white vinegar
Salt & sugar to taste

In a jar with a lid, mix light soy sauce, white vinegar, sugar and salt. Add the sliced chillies and set the mixture aside for at least 2 hours or preferably overnight. Serve as an accompaniment for wantan mee (see page 92). Keep in the fridge for up to 1-2 weeks.

Crispy fried chicken skin

Crispy fried shallots & garlic bits

CRISPY FRIED CHICKEN SKIN

I use crispy fried chicken skin as a garnish. This is an alternative to the crispy pork lard that many hawkers in Penang use (especially in wantan mee).

250g chicken skin either thinly sliced or cut into little cubes Salt to taste 3-5 tablespoons cooking oil	Season the chicken skin with salt evenly. In a pan heat some oil over medium heat. Add the seasoned skin and let it crisp up and turn golden. Make sure the skin is thoroughly crisped and remove from pan onto some paper towels. Once cooled, store the crispy skins in an airtight container.

CHICKEN STOCK

2 chicken carcasses (cut into small pieces if desired) 10 white peppercorns 2 spring onions 1 large onion 3 litres water	In a big pot, bring water to a boil. Smash the white peppercorns to release its flavours. Add the chicken carcasses, spring onions, onions and smashed peppercorns into the boiling water. Simmer for 1 hour. Strain the stock. If you prefer a richer stock bring the strained stock back to a boil and continue to simmer to reduce it. Store in a glass jar for 1-2 weeks. You could also freeze it and store it for longer. Best to freeze it in batches, so that you will only defrost the amount you will need instead of the whole amount.

GARLIC OIL & BITS

20 garlic cloves finely minced 250ml cooking oil	In a pan heat up the oil and fry the garlic over a low heat until fragrant and golden. Pour the garlic and oil into a glass jar and set aside to cool. The garlic oil can be stored and used within a week. The garlic bits could also be kept separately in an airtight jar for about 1-2 weeks in a cool dry place.

SHALLOT/ONION PASTE

Much like the garlic paste, shallot paste is primarily used as a foundation for making curry and other types of pastes. You would not eat shallot paste raw.

20 shallots (or 4 onions) 5 garlic cloves 3 thumb-sized ginger 3-5 tablespoons of water	In a food processor, blitz all the ingredients with a little water. Keep in an airtight jar in the fridge for up to 2-3 weeks.

SHALLOT OIL & CRISPY FRIED SHALLOTS

When making fried shallots, it's best to slice the shallots as finely as possible. This will ensure that they turn out crispy. Make these in big batch and store them in an airtight container. They keep for up to 3-4 weeks in the fridge.

30 shallots, thinly sliced 8-10 tablespoons cooking oil	In a pan of oil add sliced shallots while the oil is at room temperature. Ensure the shallots are evenly coated with oil so that these cook evenly. Once the sliced shallots start to turn light golden brown, turn off the heat to avoid burning these. Scoop out the fried shallots onto a kitchen towel to soak up the excess oil. When these have cooled, store them in an airtight container. When the remaining oil in the pan is completely cool, pour it through a fine sieve into an airtight jar. The aromatic shallot oil can be used to make chee cheong fun, muar chee (see pages 46 and 138 respectively) and many other things.

SAMBAL SOTONG KERING (CUTTLEFISH SAMBAL)

Essentially a Mamak influenced dish, used as a condiment and as a sauce base for mee goreng and mee rebus. This sambal is usually made spicy to enhance the flavours of these noodle dishes and is also a great accompaniment with steamed white rice or nasi lemak. You can make this ahead of time and store in an airtight container in the fridge for a few days. Heat it up to serve.

2 dried cuttlefish soaked in water overnight, washed and cut into bite-sized strips (alternatively you can use fresh cuttlefish or squid)
100g peanuts, toasted (optional)
5 ladles sambal tumis (see page 20)
300ml water
Salt & sugar to taste
2-3 tablespoons cooking oil

Finely grind the toasted peanuts in a food processor and set aside. In a pot heat up some oil, and gently fry the sambal tumis. Add the soaked cuttlefish and stir to coat with sambal evenly. Loosen with water and bring it to a boil. Let it simmer on a low to medium heat with the lid on for 45 minutes to 1 hour or until the cuttlefish is soft. Don't forget to stir occasionally. Add the ground peanuts and mix well. Season with sugar and salt to taste and allow simmer for another 10-15 minutes. When the cuttlefish is thoroughly cooked and tender, remove from heat. Serve immediately with nasi lemak (see page 78) or mee goreng (see page 72) store in air tight container for up to 2-3 days in the fridge.

Sambal tumis

CHICKEN CHAR SIEW (BARBECUED CHICKEN)

This is typically used as garnish in many street food dishes including, wantan mee and char hor fun. This is pretty easy to make but doesn't last for too long as it usually gets eaten really fast!

2 chicken breasts
4 pieces Chinese fermented red beancurd
1 teaspoon garlic paste
4 tablespoons of hoisin sauce
1 teaspoon five spice powder
2 tablespoons honey
2 tablespoons soy sauce
1 tablespoon dark soy sauce
1 teaspoon sesame oil
Ground white pepper to taste

COOK'S NOTE
In this recipe, I've used red bean curds as colouring for the meat, it also adds a little extra flavour. If you are unable to get hold of fermented red bean curd, you could use red food colouring to achieve that distinctive red hue of 'char siew'.

In a large bowl, mash the fermented red beancurd. Add hoisin sauce, garlic paste, five spice powder, ground white pepper, honey, soy sauce, dark soy sauce and sesame oil. Mix the marinade well. Loosen with water if the marinade is too thick. Add chicken breasts and coat them well. Cover the bowl with cling film and marinade overnight in the fridge.

Line a baking tray with aluminium foil or baking paper. Pour the remaining marinade into a small pot and bring it to a boil. Allow it to simmer until the glaze thickens. Remove from heat and set aside.

Preheat the oven to 180 degrees Celsius. Roast the chicken breasts for 45 minutes. Remove the chicken breasts every 15 minutes and glaze with the extra marinade on both sides. Put the chicken breasts back into the oven and continue to roast and glaze for another two rounds.

Char siew is usually served as a garnish with rice or noodle dishes and can also be a main served with steamed white rice and green vegetables such as pak choy.

LITTLE BITES

LOR BAK

SERVES: 4

The word lor bak comes from the two components of the dish: the thick starchy dipping sauce (lor) and the meat (bak). Lor bak is traditionally made out of pork but the chicken version is very well known as well. The main seasoning in the making of lor bak is Chinese five-spice powder which gives the meat a rather reddish-purple colour. The marinated meat is then wrapped in beancurd sheets which give it a crunchy texture after deep frying. Lor bak is sold as a street food snack usually along with sliced cucumbers, fried beancurd, prawn fritters (see page 36) and other accompaniments.

Lor bak is served with two options of dips: the thick starchy dip with a flavouring of Chinese five spice powder and soy sauce, and a chilli sauce. Alternatively, you could dip these 'crispy-on-the-outside-and-tender-on-the-inside' snacks in plum sauce or barbeque sauce.

MEAT FILLING
300g chicken fillet, cut into thin strips
5 water chestnuts, cut into thin strips (fresh or from a can)
3 shallots, thinly sliced
1 ½ teaspoon five-spice powder
1 tablespoon oyster sauce
1 teaspoon sesame oil
2 tablespoons corn starch or tapioca flour
Ground white pepper to taste
Salt & sugar to taste

SEALING PASTE
1 tablespoon flour mixed with 100ml water

Dried beancurd sheets (cut into squares of 15cm x 15cm)
Cooking oil for deep frying
Chilli sauce for dipping (see page 21)

LOR SAUCE
300ml chicken stock (see page 23)
1 teaspoon Chinese five spice powder
2 tablespoons dark soy sauce
1 tablespoon light soy sauce
2 tablespoons corn flour mixed with 200ml water
1 egg white, beaten
Salt & sugar to taste

Mix all the meat filling and meat seasoning ingredients in a large bowl and marinate it for at least 1-2 hours or overnight in the fridge.

Lay out the beancurd sheet and scoop about 2 tablespoons of filling in one corner into a cylinder shape. Roll up the ingredients and seal the end of the beancurd sheet with the sealing paste. Press to seal the roll and twist the ends of the roll like a candy wrapper.

Heat your oil in a deep pan to a medium heat, and deep fry your lor bak for 3-5 minutes until golden. Dry off on a paper towel.

To serve, slice the lor bak diagonally in the middle and serve with a side of chilli sauce and lor sauce for dipping.

LOR SAUCE
In a small pan over a medium heat, mix the chicken stock, five spice powder, dark soy sauce, light soy sauce. Add sugar and dissolve the sugar gently over the heat. Add the cornflour and water mix. Stir gently. Once combined and thickened, add the egg white. Heat through the sauce but be careful not to allow it to boil. Season with salt and sugar to your preferred taste. Remove from heat and set aside to cool before storing in an airtight container.

Fresh Spring Rolls

POPIAH BASAH

SERVES: 4

Popiah or fresh spring rolls, are not deep fried like the usual spring rolls you get from Chinese restaurants or the frozen varieties from supermarkets. Popiah are of Hokkien origin and what makes these Penang spring rolls different from their Thai or Vietnamese counterparts is the juicy filling and jicama gravy.

JICAMA FILLING
2 shallots, chopped
2 garlic cloves, chopped
1 tablespoon tauchu paste (preserved soybean paste)
1 large sengkuang (jicama), grated, rinsed and drained
1 carrot, grated
250ml water
Ground white pepper to taste
Salt & sugar to taste
2-3 tablespoons cooking oil

10-12 spring roll wrappers
3-5 Chinese lettuce leaves or iceberg lettuce leaves
2 pieces of firm beancurd, fried and thinly sliced
200g prawns, peeled, boiled and diced
2 tablespoons fried shallots
3 tablespoons sweet flour sauce (or hoisin sauce)
3 tablespoons chilli sauce (see page 21)

Heat up oil in a wok, fry the garlic and shallots until fragrant. Add bean paste and fry until fragrant. Add the grated jicama and carrot and cook until translucent. Add water to loosen the mix and season with salt, sugar and white pepper. Place the cooked jicama aside and save the gravy.

To assemble the popiah start by spreading the sweet flour sauce and/or chilli sauce on the popiah wrapper. Place a lettuce leaf in the centre then pile on the bean curd, jicama, prawns, and fried shallots. Roll it up like a burrito and cut the popiah into two halves in the centre. To serve, scoop the hot jicama gravy over the cut popiah.

Deep-Fried Spring Rolls

POPIAH GORENG

SERVES: 4

Stir-fried shredded jicama with carrots and long beans, encased in thin spring roll wrappers then deep fried to perfection. This is a real favourite and can also be enjoyed by vegetarians. It is best eaten while it's hot with spicy chilli sauce. In our family, we also like to dip and soak popiah goreng in laksa broth. Heavenly!

SPRING ROLL FILLING
2 shallots
1 garlic clove
1 large sengkuang (jicama) grated, rinsed and drained
2 carrots, grated
3-5 long green beans, thinly sliced
100g prawns, peeled and diced (optional)
Ground white pepper to taste
Salt & sugar to taste
2-3 tablespoons cooking oil

SEALING PASTE
1 tablespoon flour mixed with 2 tablespoons water

OTHER INGREDIENTS
10 - 12 spring roll wrappers
Cooking oil for deep frying
Chilli sauce for dipping (see page 21)

Heat up oil in a wok. Fry the garlic and shallots until fragrant. Add prawns, jicama, green beans and carrots into the wok. Season with salt, sugar and white pepper to taste. Keep stirring for 10–15 minutes until all the ingredients are cooked. Once cooked, turn off the heat. Set aside to cool.

Heap 2 tablespoons full of filling in the centre of the popiah wrapper. Fold in the two sides and roll up the popiah into a cigar shape. Seal the ends with the sealing paste. Heat up oil in a pan and deep fry the popiah over a medium heat until golden. Serve while hot with homemade chilli sauce.

HALF-BOILED EGGS & KAYA TOAST

SERVES: 2

Growing up, my mum used to make half-boiled eggs for breakfast during the weekend. You can find this simple but delicious breakfast in most Chinese kopitiams (coffee shop) during breakfast time. The kaya spread (also known as coconut jam) is made out of coconut milk, palm sugar and eggs. The tradition of adding light soy sauce and a pinch of ground white pepper to the eggs is something you cannot, I repeat CANNOT skip.

COOK'S NOTE
Homemade kaya tends to be chunkier than store-bought kaya which is made with preservatives and is usually stickier and gooier. It takes effort to make kaya and with some love and patience it is possible to achieve a smooth texture.

4 eggs
Light soy sauce to taste
Ground white pepper to taste
4 slices of toast
2 knobs of butter
4 tablespoons of kaya (coconut jam)

KAYA
3 eggs whole
2 egg yolks
1 cup white sugar
4 tablespoons white sugar
300ml coconut milk
3 pandan leaves, knotted

The perfect half-boiled egg starts with boiling a pot of water then turning off the heat. Immediately place your eggs into the pot of boiled water and make sure the eggs are fully submerged. Cover the pot with a lid and leave the eggs to cook in the residual heat for 7 minutes. If you want your eggs to be slightly firmer, you can leave these for up to 10 minutes.

Remove the eggs from the pot and submerge these in a bowl of cold water. Crack two eggs per individual in small bowls or mugs. Use a small teaspoon to scrape out the contents. Add a splash of light soy sauce and a pinch of ground white pepper over the eggs. Make your toast and spread some kaya and add a knob of butter on top. A hot cup of coffee is the perfect accompaniment.

KAYA
Beat all the eggs and egg yolks in a mixing bowl. Add in the sugar and whisk until the sugar is dissolved. Slowly add coconut milk to the mixture. Sieve the mixture through a fine sieve into a clean mixing bowl and remove any lumps. Bring a pot of water on a stove to a simmer. Place your mixing bowl (with the mixture) on top of the pot with simmering water to create a double-boiler/bain marie. Add in the knotted pandan leaves and stir with a wooden spoon over a small to medium heat for about 45 minutes or until the mixture thickens slightly and darkens. Continuously stir the mixture to ensure there are no lumps. Continue to stir for another 35 minutes. You are almost there!

In a separate pan, add 4 tablespoons of sugar and a little water. Heat it up over a low heat. Do not stir the mixture but lightly swirl the pan to mix the sugar and water. Cook until the mixture becomes a golden caramel (watch out not to burn the sugar!) turn off the heat and set it aside to cool for a minute. Gently pour the caramel mixture into the kaya and mix well. If you prefer your kaya darker add in another batch of caramel; kaya is usually a deep golden brown colour, almost like toffee.

When you're happy with your kaya's colour, continue to cook the mixture for another 15 minutes in the bain marie until you're happy with the consistency. Set aside the kaya to cool and bear in mind that it will continue to thicken even when it's removed from the heat (the knotted pandan leaves can be thrown away). Once cooled, pour into a jar and keep in the fridge for up to 3-4 weeks.

Prawn Fritters

CUCUR UDANG

SERVES: 4

Cucur Udang is a street food usually sold on pushcarts along the roadsides in Penang. There are three variations of cucur udang in Penang based on which local culture it is inspired by. The Ma'ay version of cucur udang are more round in shape, crunchy on the outside and soft or "empok" in the middle. The prawns are shelled and are either whole or chopped and mixed into the batter before deep-frying. Whereas the Chinese variety are crispier and wafer thin with unshelled prawns or top. The Indian or Mamak variety are mostly found in pasembur (hot salad of prawn fritters with sliced cucumbers, fried tofu and grated yambean, see page 50). They are more oblong in shape and are filled with sliced onions, spring onions and the prawns used are not shelled.

When I was growing up, my maternal grandma used to make these crunchy fritters for our afternoon snack. After some gardening activities with my grandpa, we would tuck into these crunchy golden nuggets with a cup of tea or coffee. My fondest memory of these relaxing afternoons would be my grandpa picking out the prawns from his fritters to give to me while he munched on his prawn-emptied prawn fritters.

150g raw prawns shelled, whole or cut into cubes
½ red onion, sliced thinly
2 spring onions, cut into 2cm strips
2 cups plain flour
½ teaspoon baking powder
½ teaspoon turmeric powder
½ teaspoon chilli powder
1 egg
350ml cold water
Salt & sugar to taste
Cooking oil for deep-frying

Mix all the dry ingredients in a large bowl. Crack the egg and add water gradually until the batter reaches a thick smooth consistency. Add the wet ingredients - prawns, sliced onions and spring onions - into the bowl. Mix well. In a wok or sauce pan, heat up the oil. Scoop a tablespoon of batter and gently release it into the hot oil. Fry 3 – 5 balls of cucur udang for 3 minutes on each side; don't crowd your wok or the batter won't cook through. When both sides are golden brown, remove from oil and drain on a paper towel. Serve hot with sweet chilli sauce as a condiment and a nice hot cup of tea.

Crispy Flat Bread

ROTI CANAI

SERVES: 4

Roti canai is a staple breakfast dish and its origin can be traced back to the Indian migrants who arrived on the shores of Malaya. It's a simple dough stretched very thinly to trap as much air as possible, this allows it to achieve a wafer crisp consistency when fried over ghee or oil. Once the roti is cooked, it is clapped together to give its crunchy yet fluffy texture. You can find roti canai in all mamak eateries as well as some Malay establishments. Traditionally, it is eaten with a serving of dhal or chicken curry. The crispy roti soaks up the curry gravy perfectly, releasing an explosion of flavours in every bite.

One of my fondest memories is tucking into roti canai right after my Saturday morning squash classes. Either mom or Pak Hamid (a grandfatherly figure in my childhood who used to pick and drop me off from school as both my parents were at work), would bring me to a local mamak shop to have roti canai banjir, here the word banjir refers to roti canai drenched in curry gravy instead of being served separately. Nowadays instead of the plain old roti canai, you can find these roti's stuffed with egg, cheese, banana and many other new creations.

2 cups plain wheat flour
2 tablespoons condensed milk
⅓ cup ghee (or butter)
180ml warm water
Salt & sugar to taste
Cooking oil and ghee for soaking and frying

If you are using butter instead of ghee, soften it to room temperature. Mix flour, ghee, sugar, salt, condensed milk and water in a mixing bowl. Mix and knead until the dough is formed. The dough should be sticky at this point. Dust some flour on a smooth countertop. Knead the dough for at least 10 minutes. The dough is ready once it stops sticking to your fingers. Make sure the dough is not too stiff, if it is, add more water. If it's too wet, dust lightly with more flour. Let the dough rest in the bowl for about 30-45 minutes covered with a cloth.

After the dough has rested, knead it for another 5-10 minutes. Divide the kneaded dough into 8 equal parts. Make sure the little dough balls have no creases. Smoothing the dough can be done by pinching in the sides of the dough and pulling it into the middle. Coat each piece with a little oil or ghee. Arrange these in a shallow flat surfaced bowl so that these do not touch and pour in enough cooking oil to cover these. Cover with cling film and leave them to rest for at least 1 hour or overnight in the fridge.

1. Place one dough ball on a countertop and gently press and spread the sides with the palm of your hand until it is thin enough to be able to flip.

2. Position your left hand on top of the flattened dough with the left thumb underneath, while your right hand goes underneath the flattened dough with the right thumb on top.

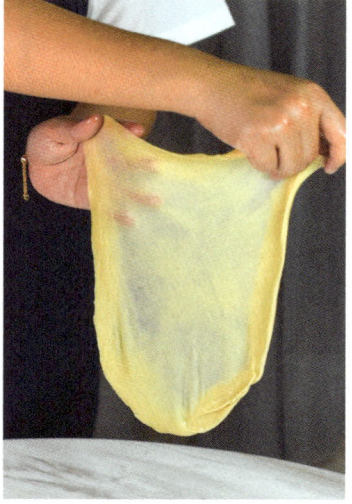

3. Lightly flip and slap the dough back onto the surface to stretch the dough. Add more ghee or oil to help with the stretching.

4. Flip and slap until you have stretched the dough out as thinly as you can, don't worry if the stretched dough has holes in it.

COOK'S NOTE
Keep extra flour near you when kneading the dough to dust your countertop easily.

5. Fold all four sides into a square and you are ready to fry the roti canai. Heat up ghee or oil in a flat surface pan. Place your envelope shaped pastry and fry until golden and flip to cook each side. Remove from heat onto a cool surface.

6. 'Clap' the sides of the roti canai together to fluff it up before serving.

   Serve with a chicken curry or dhal of your preference (see kari kapitan ayam and kari dalca on page 82 and page 85 respectively).

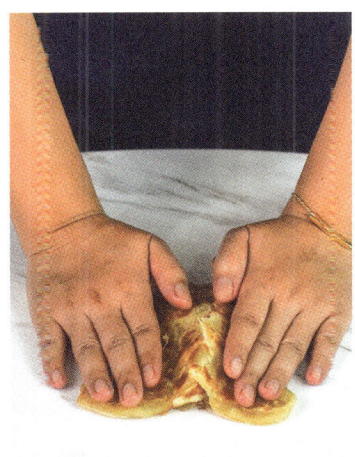

Meat-Stuffed Pancake
MURTABAK

SERVES: 4

Murtabak is an Indian-Muslim favourite and it is also made by the Malay community. It uses the thin wafer pastry of the Roti Canai as its pastry while the filling is made from spiced minced meat, onion and egg. Assembling murtabak is complex! Think of an Italian lasagne but fried till it is crispy. Two thin layers of meat and pastry will be cooked first before enclosing the cooked meaty pancake in a stretched pastry and fried to crisp. Murtabak is served hot with pink pickled onions and curry gravy. It's a balance of savoury from the murtabak with sourness from the pickled onions and spiciness of the curry that makes this snack perfect not only for snacking but also as a meal on its own.

The pastry used is similar to the roti canai recipe. The recipe starts with preparing all the essential components of the murtabak: pastry, meat filling and pink pickled onion. Then the recipe continues with the assembly of the murtabak.

Growing up, our family usually enjoy eating murtabak during the Ramadan month. Go to any Ramadan bazaar and you'll find more than one stall making these.

8 roti canai dough balls (see page 40)

MEAT FILLING
450g minced chicken
2 large onions, thinly sliced
2 garlic cloves, chopped
1 tablespoon ground coriander seed powder
1 tablespoon chilli powder
1 tablespoon turmeric powder
1 tablespoon cumin seed powder
4 eggs
Ground white pepper powder to taste
Salt to taste
2-3 tablespoons cooking oil

GARNISH
Pink pickled onions (see page 22)

Heat up oil in pan and fry the onions and garlic until fragrant. Add the spices. Finally, add the minced chicken and fry until the meat is brown. Remove from heat and set aside. Divide this into four portions for later.

ASSEMBLING & COOKING THE MURTABAK
Spread a dough ball on a countertop with ghee/butter. Stretch the dough very thinly until it is see-through then fold the stretched pastry into a 10cm square. Make four square pastries and leave the four remaining dough balls to wrap the meat filling.

Heat up ghee/butter in a pan. Fry the square pastries on both sides until golden brown. Then set them aside.

In a bowl break an egg and mix in one portion of the meat filling. Heat up ghee/butter in a pan. Spread half of the meat filling into a square shape about the same size as the square pastry, onto the pan. Place the square pastry on top of the meat filling. Spread the remaining half portion of the meat filling on top of the square pastry. When the meat filling at the bottom is cooked and brown, carefully flip to the other side to cook.

Spread a ball of dough on countertop and stretch the dough as thinly as possible. Make sure the stretched dough is at least 15cm in diameter and is see-through.

Place the meat filling with pastry in the middle of the thinly stretched pastry, then fold in the four sides like an envelope. Cook each side until golden brown. Serve while it's hot with pink pickled onions and a little curry gravy for dipping.

Oyster Omelette
OH CHIEN

SERVES: 2

There's nothing like Penang oh chien and although it is a simple delicacy to make, it is challenging to make it well. It takes plenty of experience and know-how to judge the timing and the heat to achieve the perfect consistency.

One secret to making your oh chien as authentic as the ones in most kopitiams is to line your plate with banana leaf. The heat from the freshly cooked oh chien will permeate into the banana leaf and release an aromatic flavour. Delicious! If you're ever in Penang, I highly recommend visiting the Seng Thor Coffee Shop on Carnarvon Street for a real taste of this amazing dish (you might have to queue, so be prepared!).

STARCH BATTER
80g tapioca starch flour (local oh chien sellers also use sweet potato flour)
300ml water
2 stalks Chinese chives, cut into 2cm strips
Salt to taste

OMELETTE
4 eggs
2 garlic cloves chopped finely
200g fresh oysters shelled and washed
1 teaspoon light soy sauce
1 teaspoon fish sauce
Ground white pepper to taste
1 sprig of coriander leaves
1 teaspoon of chopped chai por (preserved radish) – this is optional and if you can't find it it's fine to leave it out.
3-5 tablespoons cooking oil
Garlic chilli sauce (see page 21)

Thoroughly mix the starch batter ingredients in a bowl. Heat up some oil in a pan over a medium heat. Pour a ladle full of the starch batter into the pan. Stir the starch to cook. Crack the eggs over the cooked starch. Let the eggs cook a little before scrambling. Push the egg and starch mix to the side of the pan. Add in more oil and cook the chopped garlic until fragrant (add in the preserved radish if you are using it). Season the garlic mix with fish sauce and add the oysters. Mix everything together. Season with light soy sauce and ground white pepper to taste. Remove your oyster omelette from the pan and garnish with chopped coriander leaves. Serve piping hot with the garlic chilli sauce.

Steamed Rice Rolls with Prawn Paste

CHEE CHEONG FUN

SERVES: 4

You cannot mention Penang street food without mentioning chee cheong fun. It's a really basic delicacy but packs a punch of flavours. The flavour is mostly in the black prawn paste sauce which is a combination of hae ko (prawn paste), shallot oil and an optional chilli sauce. There's now even curry drenched chee cheong fun too!

The traditional recipe for the cheong fun or rice rolls is below, although if you're feeling lazy you can easily buy these from any Asian supermarket.

RICE ROLLS
1 cup rice flour
¼ cup wheat starch
¼ cup tapioca flour
¼ cup cornflour
⅛ teaspoon alkaline water (see page 18)
650ml water
3-5 tablespoons cooking oil

GARNISH
20 rolls chee cheong fun (steamed rice rolls)
Hae ko (black prawn paste, see page 15)
Garlic chilli sauce (see page 21)
Shallot oil (see page 24)
2 tablespoons toasted sesame seeds
Fried shallots (see page 24)

Sieve all the flour into a bowl. Add the rest of the liquid ingredients into the bowl and mix well. The mixture should be runny. Strain the mixture through a fine strainer. Leave the batter to rest for at least 30 minutes.

Grease a rectangular tray that fits into your steamer with oil. Ladle and spread a thin layer of batter onto the tray. Steam the tray in a heated steamer for 1 minute on high heat. When the batter is cooked, remove from heat. Brush the rice sheet with a thin layer of oil and roll it into a long cigar shape. Place the cooked rice roll in an oiled tray and cover to prevent it drying while you make the rest of the rolls. Add a little water into the liquid batter mix if it has become a little thick.

ASSEMBLING THE CHEE CHEONG FUN
Cut the chee cheong fun into 1cm bite-sizes and place on a plate. Drizzle a little shallot oil over the rolls. Drizzle prawn paste sauce and garlic chilli sauce to taste. Lastly, sprinkle some toasted sesame seeds and crispy fried shallots.

COOK'S NOTE
Alternatively you could serve with sambal tumis instead of garlic chilli sauce for extra oomph!

Fruit Salad with Black Prawn Paste

PENANG ROJAK

SERVES: 4

Penang rojak is essentially a fruit salad of fresh tropical fruits tossed with black prawn paste that is sweet, salty, sour and slightly spicy. Much like the salad, rojak is the word we use to describe Malaysia's diverse culture which is made up of so many different ethnic groups. We usually make or order a large portion of rojak to share as part of a main meal.

ROJAK SAUCE
3 tablespoons chilli sauce (see page 21)
1 thumb-sized belacan (shrimp paste), toasted
5 tablespoons hae ko (black prawn paste, see page 15)
½ cup castor sugar
Juice from 5 calamansi limes
100ml warm water

⅓ of a pineapple, cut into bite-sized cubes
1 guava, cut into bite-sized cubes
1 green mango, cut into bite-sized strips – best to pick a young green mango that is still crunchy
3 jambu air (water apples) cut into bite-sized pieces
1 sengkuang (jicama) cut into bite-sized strips
½ cucumber, cut into bite-sized strips
3 ambra fruits
1 tablespoon toasted peanuts, finely crushed
1 tablespoon toasted sesame seeds

In a small pan, mix all the rojak sauce ingredients; except for the calamansi lime juice, over a low to medium heat. The point of the heat is not to cook the sauce but to make it easier to mix. The end consistency should be a caramel like gooey sauce, you can always add in more water if you prefer it less gooey. Turn off heat, then add calamansi lime juice and mix well. Leave aside to cool.

In a large bowl, combine all the fruit salad ingredients. Drizzle the rojak sauce and toss well. Sprinkle crushed peanuts and sesame seeds on top to serve.

PASEMBUR

SERVES: 4

Pasembur is an Indian-Muslim delicacy, also known as Indian Rojak. It's a vegetable salad topped with a rich spice-filled peanut gravy. Aside from vegetables, pasembur also includes assorted fritters such as prawn fritters, flour fritters, fried tofu and sometimes fried fishcakes which add another layer of texture and taste.

I have many happy memories of going for pasembur as a child usually right after a trip to the bank on Beach Street with mom or a fabric shopping spree at the Chowrasta bazaar with my maternal grandma. Every memory – no matter the stall – always goes back to the thick, spicy peanut gravy and the crispiness of the fried fritters. The perfect combination of textures.

SWEET SPICY PEANUT GRAVY
3 garlic cloves
8-10 shallots
3-5 dried red chillies soaked in water
2 thumb-sized belacan (shrimp paste) toasted
1 teaspoon tamarind pulp mixed in 100ml water
125g peanuts, toasted and finely crushed
1 sweet potato, boiled
800ml water
Salt & sugar to taste
3 – 5 tablespoons cooking oil

1 cucumber, cut into thin strips
1 sengkuang (jicama) cut into thin strips
2 fish cakes, fried and cut into bite-sizes
2 potatoes, medium-sized boiled, deep fried and cut into bite-sizes
2 firm tofu, fried and cut into bite-sizes
4 prawn fritters cut into bite-sized pieces (see page 36)

GRAVY
In a food processor blitz garlic, shallots, soaked dried red chillies and dried shrimp paste into a paste. In a pot heat up oil and fry the paste until aromatic.

Add the sweet potatoes and some water into the food processor. Then add the sweet potato mixture to the fragrant paste in the pot. Add in tamarind juice and crushed peanuts.

Simmer the mixture over medium heat for 15-20 minutes. Salt and sugar to taste. Set aside to prepare the rest of the ingredients.

ASSEMBLING THE PASEMBUR
On a sharing platter, scatter the cucumber and jicama, followed by the potatoes, fish cake, tofu and pieces of prawn. Top with a generous ladle of the spicy sweet peanut gravy and enjoy!

Chinese Pasembur
CHEH HU

SERVES: 4

The Chinese version of the Pasembur is lighter and sweeter in taste compared to the spicy Mamak version. It is known as cheh hu. It has all the components of the Mamak pasembur however, the gravy is not as spicy and has a sweet-sour taste thanks to the addition of plum sauce (a Chinese pantry must have).

SWEET SOUR SAUCE
1 sweet potato, medium sized
2 tablespoons chilli paste (see page 20)
5 tablespoons plum sauce
800ml water
2 tablespoons cooking oil
Salt & sugar to taste

FLOUR FRITTERS
½ cup tapioca flour
½ cup rice flour
1 egg
300ml water
Salt & sugar to taste

Prawn fritters (as many as you like) sliced into bite-sized pieces (see page 36)
3 pieces of fried beancurd, deep fried and cut into bite-sized cubes
1 cucumber, medium sized grated or cut into diagonal strips
1 sengkuang (jicama), medium sized grated or cut in to diagonal strips
250g cuttlefish, boiled or steamed and cut into bite-sized diagonal pieces (optional)
1 tablespoon toasted sesame seeds

Boil or steam the sweet potatoes. When these are cooked, set them aside to cool before peeling the skin off. In a food processor, blitz the sweet potatoes with plum sauce and water. In a pan, heat up some oil and saute the chilli paste until aromatic.

Transfer the sweet potato mixture into a pan and bring it to a boil then simmer over medium heat. Season with sugar and salt to taste. Once the consistency is thick and runny set it aside to cool. This is best eaten while it's still warm.

FLOUR FRITTERS
In a bowl mix all the flour with egg and water. Sugar and salt to taste. Mix the batter until smooth.

In a pan, heat up enough oil for deep frying. Scoop the batter and fry over medium heat until it becomes a thin crispy wafer. The crispy fritters can be stored in an airtight container for up to a week. To serve break the fritters into chunky pieces and scatter on the rest of the pasembur ingredients.

ASSEMBLING THE CHEH HU
Place and toss all the cut ingredients onto a serving platter or plate. Dollop a generous amount of sweet sour sauce on top. Add a final sprinkling of sesame seeds. You may also serve with some chilli sauce for added heat (see page 21).

OTAK-OTAK

SERVES: 4

Otak-otak is a Nyonya dish usually served with rice and other dishes, but it can also be enjoyed on its own. Otak-otak is a steamed fish parcel infused with aromatic spices and coconut milk. The wrapper is usually made of daun kaduk (wild pepper leaves) as well as banana leaves.

For a long time during my childhood, otak-otak freaked me out as otak in Malay means brain. So like most kids I took this literally! I have to confess that I also found the fishy smell a bit off putting. However, smells that used to make me nauseous, now make me salivate so I guess the older you get the more refined your palate becomes! Even its soft texture doesn't bother me anymore; I think as I get older I prefer more 'digestion-friendly' textures. I guess I should never say never!

SPICE PASTE
3-5 fresh red chillies
2 stalks lemongrass
3 kafir lime leaves, remove the entire stalk and slice finely
3 thumb-sized galangal
1 thumb-sized fresh turmeric root
2 tablespoons onion/shallot paste (see page 24)
1 thumb-sized belacan (shrimp paste) toasted
5 buah keras (candlenuts)
150ml water

250g white fish fillet
100ml coconut milk
2 eggs
2 teaspoons tapioca flour
Ground white pepper to taste
Salt & sugar to taste

25 daun kaduk (wild pepper leaves)
20 banana leaf squares, washed and flamed over a fire to soften
20 bamboo toothpicks

In a food processor (or mortar and pestle) blitz all the spice paste ingredients into a paste. Roughly chop the fish fillets into squares. Mix the fish and spice paste in a mixing bowl. Add in the coconut milk, eggs. Thinly slice 5 daun kaduk and add to the fish paste mixture. Season with white pepper, sugar and salt to taste. Marinate for at least 45 minutes or overnight.

To wrap the fish paste, start by placing one wild pepper leaf in the centre of a banana leaf square. Scoop 2-3 heaped teaspoons of the fish paste into the centre. Bring together both ends of the banana leaf, pinch and fold the top of the leaf to seal the parcel. On the opposite ends of the banana leaf pinch it together and secure it with a toothpick. Place the sealed fish parcels into a steamer and steam for 10-20 minutes. Serve while it's hot with steamed jasmine rice.

COOK'S NOTE
Scald the banana leaves over direct fire or hot boiling water to make it more pliable.

Taro/Yam Cake

OR KUIH

SERVES: 4

Yam Kuih or locally known as Or Kuih is a steamed compact and sticky kuih made of the root vegetable taro or locally called yam. The kuih or cake is served with a generous topping of fried dried shrimps and shallots with chilli sauce to dip in. There's an art to selecting and cooking the yam to achieve that fluffiness that isn't too mushy.

300g yam/taro, skinned, cut into cubes
175g rice flour
625ml water
½ tablespoon cornflour
2 garlic cloves, finely minced
3 shallots, minced
1 teaspoon Chinese five-spice powder
3-5 tablespoons cooking oil
Ground white pepper to taste
Salt to taste

GARNISH
2 tablespoons dried shrimps, soaked
2 tablespoons fried shallots (see page 24)
1 stalk spring onion, finely sliced
1 red chilli, finely chopped
Chilli sauce (see page 21)

In a mixing bowl, mix rice flour, cornflour and water.

In a wok, heat up oil and fry the minced garlic and shallots until golden and fragrant. Add the yam/taro, Chinese five-spice powder and white pepper. Fry to mix everything well and season with salt to taste. Add the flour batter and continue to stir continuously over a low heat until the mixture thickens.

Grease bowl or tin for steaming and pour the cooked batter into it. The height of the cake should be around 3 – 5cm. Steam the cake over high heat for about 30 – 40 minutes until the cake is set. Leave it to cool for a few hours before serving.

Before serving, dry fry the dried shrimps until golden and aromatic. In a food processor blitz the fried shrimps to rough pieces.

To serve, generously sprinkle fried dried shrimps, fried shallots, red chilli and spring onion onto the or kuih. Cut the steamed cake into rectangular individual slices. Serve with chilli sauce as a dipping sauce.

Steamed Vegetable Dumplings

CHAI KUIH

SERVES: 4

Chai kuih is a steamed vegetable dumpling which is usually very popular during Chinese New Year. I have included the recipes for two different fillings – yambean filling and Chinese chives filling.

DUMPLING SKIN
1 ½ cups & 1 tablespoon potato flour
1 ¼ cups tapioca flour
1 cup glutinous rice flour
500ml hot water
60ml cooking oil

JICAMA FILLING
2 garlic cloves
3 tablespoons dried shrimps, soaked and coarsely minced
3 tablespoons udang geragau (krill) - optional
1 jicama, grated
1 large carrot, grated
200ml water
2 tablespoons cooking oil
Ground white pepper to taste
Salt & sugar to taste

CHINESE CHIVES FILLING
2 garlic cloves
3 tablespoons dried shrimps, soaked and coarsely minced
8-10 stalks Chinese chives, roughly chopped
2 tablespoons cooking oil
Ground white pepper to taste
Salt to taste
Garlic oil (see page 24)
Chilli sauce (see page 21)

DUMPLING SKINS
In a mixing bowl, mix all the flour with oil and gradually add boiling water while stirring continuously. Stir until the mixture is pliable. Set aside for the dough to cool down.

Once the dough is cool, grease your hands with a little oil and divide the dough to four equal portions. Dust your table top with tapioca flour to roll the dough into thin sheets. Cut into round discs, about 7.5cm in diameter with a cutter.

JICAMA FILLING
In a pan heat up some oil and fry the garlic until fragrant. Add the soaked dried shrimps and fry until aromatic. Then add the grated jicama and carrots. Fry the mixture until the jicama is translucent while gradually adding water. Once the jicama and carrots are almost dry, season to taste with white pepper, sugar and salt. Remove from pan and set aside to cool.

CHINESE CHIVES FILLING
In a pan heat up some oil and fry the garlic until aromatic. Add the soaked dried shrimps and fry until fragrant. Lower the heat and add chives. Stir and season to taste with pepper and salt. Stir for less than 5 minutes and turn off the heat. Remove from pan and set aside to cool.

WRAPPING THE DUMPLINGS
Scoop a tablespoon of filling into the centre of the dumpling skin. Pinch together the sides of the dough into a tiny bag-like shape.

Arrange the dumplings as you make them on a greased steaming plate/tray. Steam the dumplings over high heat for 7 - 10 minutes or until the dumpling skins are translucent. To serve, remove the dumplings from the steamer and drizzle with garlic oil and serve with chilli sauce for dipping.

Cuttlefish Salad

SOTONG KANGKUNG

SERVES: 2

Sotong kangkung is a popular snack among the Chinese and Malays in Penang (it's called ju hu eng chai in Hokkien). This is a simple dish but may not seem appealing to those unaccustomed to the taste. The cuttlefish and kangkung (water convolvulus) are topped with a sweet caramel-like black prawn paste gravy and crushed toasted peanuts. In our family, we would usually have sotong kangkung as an appetiser at dinner time.

SWEET BLACK PRAWN PASTE SAUCE
¼ cup hae ko (black prawn paste, see page 15)
½ cup of gula Melaka or brown sugar
1 thumb-sized belacan (shrimp paste) toasted
1 tablespoon dark soy sauce
250ml water
1 teaspoon tamarind pulp mixed with 100ml of water soaked and strained
Salt to taste

1 large brown cuttlefish
8-10 stalks kangkung (water convolvulus)
2 tablespoons peanuts, toasted and crushed
2 tablespoons toasted sesame seeds
Chilli sauce (see page 21)

Simmer the palm sugar, hae ko and water in a pot until the sugar is dissolved. Strain the sugar syrup. Add back the strained sugar syrup into the pot and add the rest of the ingredients. Simmer the mixture over a low heat while stirring until the mixture is a thick syrup.

Clean and cut the cuttlefish into bite-size slices. Wash and cut the kangkung into 3-5cm lengths. Boil the cuttlefish slices in water for 20-30 minutes until tender. Remove from pot and strain in a colander to remove excess water. Blanch kangkung leaves in the same pot of boiling water for 5 minutes, until the leaves turn dark green.

To serve, place the blanched and drained kangkung on a large plate followed by the cuttlefish. Top it with a generous amount of sweet black prawn paste sauce along with a little chilli sauce and a final sprinkling of toasted crushed peanuts and sesame seeds.

Malaysian Street Skewers Hotpot

LOK LOK

SERVES: 4 - 6

If you walk down the streets of George Town in the evening, you are bound to come across a street food cart displaying a wonderous assortment of food on skewers. These are called lok lok which means to dip and is a street food rendition of the steamboat or hotpot.

Steamboat is traditionally eaten on the eve of Chinese New Year and is typically a big pot of bubbling soup - sometimes holding two varieties, one a flavourful broth and the other a spicy one. Surrounding the bubbling pot are assortments of meat, vegetables and noodles or anything else you could think of that would taste great cooked in the broth. Steamboat is a communal meal. Having a steamboat is all about spending time with your fellow diners, from deciding what to cook in the communal broth, to actually cooking and dividing who gets what and so forth, a meal like this can last for hours throughout the night.

Lok lok has all the same components except the sitting around for hours as it was adapted for the streets with all the convenience of grabbing a meal on the go. Bamboo skewers with coloured markers pierce bite-sized food to help the vendors categorise and price the food selection. The type of food on offer ranges from fishballs, meatballs, beancurd sheets, wantan dumplings and fresh seafood including cockles, prawns and squid. There are plenty of vegetables including mushrooms, Chinese greens and meat such chicken, pork and pork offal.

There isn't much cooking involved in lok lok so the crucial part is the dipping sauces. Feel free to use all kinds of meat and vegetables that you enjoy and just have fun with your dinner guests.

SPICY GARLIC SAUCE WITH DRIED SHRIMPS

2 tablespoons of dried shrimps, washed and soaked until soft
8 red chillies (deseeded if you want it to be less spicy)
3 garlic cloves
1 tablespoon white vinegar
Sugar to taste

SPICY GARLIC SAUCE WITH DRIED SHRIMPS

Toast the dried shrimps over medium heat in a small pan until these are aromatic and slightly crisped. In food processor, blitz the toasted dried shrimps, chillies, garlic cloves, vinegar and sugar. It can be stored in airtight jar for up to 2 weeks in the fridge.

SATAY SAUCE (PEANUT SAUCE)

500g peanuts (with or without the skin is fine, personally I prefer skinned peanuts)
8 dried red chillies deseeded, soaked in hot water (alternatively you can use fresh red chillies)
8 shallots or 2 red onions, roughly chopped
3-4 garlic cloves
1 thumb-sized ginger
1 thumb-sized galangal
1 lemongrass stalk
¼ cup gula Melaka (palm sugar) or brown sugar
1 teaspoon tamarind pulp mixed with 100ml water
1 thumb-sized dried shrimp paste (belacan) toasted
300ml water
3-5 tablespoons cooking oil
Salt to taste

SWEET SOUR SAUCE

½ cup of Hoisin sauce
⅓ cup of plum sauce
3 tablespoons sesame oil
Mix all ingredients in a small bowl.

LOK LOK SKEWERS

A generous pot of chicken broth (see page 23)
300g chicken slices
300g beef slices
500g prawns (optional to shell)
300g cuttlefish or squid, cleaned and cut into bite-sizes
300g meatballs
300g fishballs
250g crabmeat sticks
200g cockles, cleaned and shelled
15 quail eggs, boiled and shelled
10 fried beancurd sheets, cut into bite-sizes
300g assortment of mushrooms (enoki, button, oyster, etc)
10 cobs baby corn
300g choy sum greens, cut into bite-sizes
1 packet of bamboo skewers

SATAY SAUCE (PEANUT SAUCE)

In a small pan, toast the peanuts until aromatic and slightly brown. Remove from heat and let these cool for a bit. Blitz the peanuts in to coarse dust.

Prepare the spice paste by blitzing the soaked dried chillies, shallots, garlic, ginger, galangal, belacan and lemongrass in a food processor. Set aside.

In a pot, heat up the oil. Pour in the spice paste and sauté until fragrant and the oil has separated which takes about 20-25 minutes on medium high heat while continuously stirring. Add in the ground peanuts. Add a little water to loosen the mixture. Let it simmer for about 10-15 minutes. Add palm sugar, tamarind with water and salt to taste. Continue to simmer until the oil "floats" to the surface of the peanut sauce and the consistency thickens. Remove from heat. To serve, ladle into a large bowl so that guests can spoon a little onto their own plate to use as a dipping sauce.

LOK LOK SKEWERS

Push 3-5 pieces of each ingredient through a bamboo skewer. Once these are ready set aside. On a portable stove, bring the chicken broth to boil and allow to simmer. Your guests can select their skewers and cook these by dipping the skewers into the simmering broth. Set aside individual bowls of sauces for each guest or use individual plates to spoon the sauces onto.

Malaysian Sloppy Street Burger

RAMLY BURGER

SERVES: 2

This Malaysian icon can be found all over the streets of Penang and Malaysia and takes its name from the famous burger patty brand. My childhood memories of eating Ramly burgers are the sloppy sauces dripping all over me; it's not a pretty or sexy meal but an extremely satisfying one. My favourite customized burger order as child (and adult!) was half and half – a beef and chicken patty, hold the veggies, no chilli sauce only mayonnaise and a fried egg.

The unique part of the Ramly burger is the thin egg wrap that hugs the meat patty. As you bite into it, the sauce oozes out of the egg casing – an explosion of flavours as the meat patty is seasoned with spices to give it that truly Malaysian flavour. This recipe is so easy to make at home. Don't be afraid to be generous with your chilli sauce and mayonnaise.

800g ground beef or ground chicken (this recipe makes two generous burgers)
1 tablespoon curry powder
2 tablespoons Worcestershire sauce (local burger stalls use Maggi seasoning sauce)
Ground white pepper to taste
Salt to taste
2 soft burger buns
4 eggs
1 tomato, medium sized and sliced
1 romaine lettuce
2 slices of cheese of choice
2 tablespoons butter
2 tablespoons mayonnaise
2 tablespoons bottled chilli sauce or tomato ketchup

Season the meat with salt to taste then divide the minced beef into half portions. Shape each into individual medallions. Slightly flatten them.

Melt a little butter in a flat surfaced pan. Cut your soft burger buns into half and toast them inside down on the melted butter until golden brown. Remove from pan and set aside on a plate.

Melt a little more butter into the pan over medium heat. Place the beef patties onto the hot melted butter. Sprinkle some curry powder and ground white pepper on the patties. Add a dash of Worcestershire sauce. Flip the patties and sprinkle with curry powder, ground white pepper and a dash of Worcestershire sauce. Cook the patties on each side for about 3-5 minutes until these are cooked through. Remove the patties.

With the remaining butter grease on the pan, crack two eggs onto the hot pan and gently spread to make a thin omelette. Let the omelette cook through for about 2-3 minutes. Once the omelette is firm, place one cooked meat patty in the middle of the omelette. Wrap up the patty with the omelette then flip the parcel to seal it. Remove from pan and place it on your toasted bun layered with lettuce pieces, sliced tomatoes and a slice of cheese. Finish off with a generous amount of mayonnaise and chilli sauce.

RICE & NOODLES

PENANG ASSAM LAKSA

SERVES: 4

In Malaysia, there are a few variations of laksa, a noodle soaked in seafood broth, but I would definitely say that Penang assam laksa triumphs above all. This sour fishy noodle broth was made popular by the Peranakan community of Penang but its origins are Malay.

Growing up my mother had a hard time making me eat seafood as I was born a carnivore, it took years before I could eat a bowl of laksa. After I finished my first steaming bowl, all I could think was, "Why did I wait so long?!"

In Penang, you can find assam laksa in almost any hawker centre, but there are few that can claim to be the very best. My favourite stall is a tiny little kopitiam in Taman Emas run by two sisters. Since I'm not always able to visit this hidden treasure of a stall for a golden bowl of bliss, I decided to recreate the dish at home. I find the balance of sour, sweet and spicy flavours of assam laksa most appealing, like everything else in life, balance is important.

BROTH PASTE
8-10 shallots
3 garlic cloves
2 stalks of lemongrass, bruised with the back of a knife
1 thumb-sized galangal
5 fresh red chillies, deseeded for less heat
5 dried red chillies, soaked
1 thumb-sized belacan (dried shrimp paste) toasted

BROTH
350g ikan kembung (Asian mackerel)
2 litres water
1 stalk of lemongrass bruised with the back of a knife
1 teaspoon tamarind pulp mixed with 100ml water
3 pieces of asam keping (tamarind peel)
3-5 sprigs daun kesom (laksa leaves)
Salt & sugar to taste
400g fresh laksa noodles blanched

FRESH CONDIMENTS
½ cucumber, sliced into thin strips
¾ pineapple, sliced into thin strips
1 onion, thinly sliced
1 torch bunga kantan (torch ginger flower) finely chopped
1 fresh red chilli, thinly sliced (this is optional)
3-5 sprigs mint leaves
Hae ko (prawn paste sauce, see page 15)

In a food processor, blitz all the broth paste ingredients into a smooth paste. Gut and clean the fish. Bring water to a boil and add the lemongrass and fish. Boil for 5 minutes or until the fish is just cooked. Remove the fish and leave aside to cool. Once cooled, debone and flake. Strain the fish stock into a clean pot then add the broth paste to the stock. Simmer over low heat for 30 minutes until the gravy is aromatic.

Add the fish flakes, tamarind pulp water, tamarind peel, laksa leaves and the lemongrass stalk. Bring the broth to a boil. Season to taste with salt and sugar. If you have the patience, let the broth simmer on a low heat for about 20 – 30 minutes longer for all the ingredients to infuse each other and make the broth taste better.

To serve the laksa, place laksa noodles in a bowl and top with the fresh condiments before ladling the fish broth over the bowl. Serve with a spoonful of prawn paste sauce.

MEE GORENG MAMAK

SERVES: 2

Predominantly made by Indian Muslims, mee goreng mamak has now become a staple food consumed by all. The secret to its starchy and melt-in-your-mouth texture is the incorporation of boiled potatoes into the noodle mix. I cannot stress enough to never leave out this humble but impactful spud. I think the best mee goreng is served at the Bangkok Lane kopitiam, a local Chinese coffee shop. Perhaps I'm biased as it was always a treat my mom would take me for after my Saturday squash lessons when I was in high school. My favourite side order? Extra sotong, but not too spicy please!

SEASONING SAUCE
2 tablespoons light soy sauce
2 tablespoons dark soy sauce
2 tablespoons chilli sauce (see page 21)
3 tablespoons tomato ketchup
Salt to taste
3-4 tablespoons water

NOODLES & CONDIMENTS
2 garlic cloves, finely chopped
3 tablespoons chilli paste (see page 20)
2 stalks choy sum (Chinese flowering cabbage) cut into 2cm strips
400g yellow noodles, blanched
1 piece of beancurd, fried to golden, cut into bite-sized cubes
1 large potato, boiled and cut into cubes
2 eggs
1 handful beansprouts
2 stalks spring onions
2-3 tablespoons cooking oil

GARNISH
Fried shallots (see page 24)
1 fresh red chilli, sliced diagonally
2 calamansi limes, cut into half
Sambal sotong kering (see page 25)

Heat oil in a wok. Fry the garlic and chilli paste until fragrant. Add noodles and fry over high heat for a few seconds, stirring continuously. Add seasoning sauce into the wok and stir. Add the beancurd and potato cubes. Mix well.

Lower the heat and make a well in the middle of the noodles, add a little oil and crack in the eggs. Scramble the eggs and cook for a few seconds. Add in greens and fry for a few seconds. Finally add beansprouts and spring onion and stir.

To serve garnish with fried shallots, red chilli and a squeeze of calamansi lime over the noodles (this crucial step, makes all the difference). Finally, don't forget your dollop of sambal sotong kering!

> **COOK'S NOTE**
> *The secret to any fried noodles or fried rice is, after mixing everything well, leave it alone over high heat to let it char (caramelise not burn) at the bottom. Once you smell and hear it, make one last stir and turn heat off. Serve immediately.*

Chinese Prawn Noodles

PENANG HOKKIEN MEE

SERVES: 4

Hokkien mee is a fiery coloured prawn broth with mixture of vermicelli rice noodles and yellow noodles. The secret to a good Hokkien mee is the broth and it is best prepared a day earlier before serving, to allow the flavours of the ingredients to blend with one another. Originally, pork bones are used in the making of the broth. But you can easily yield similar results from chicken bones.

BROTH
10 dried chillies, soaked
10 shallots
3 garlic cloves
800g prawns with shells and heads still attached (the meat is used as a garnish)
3 litres water
1 whole chicken, bones cut into pieces
1 chicken breast (to be shredded and used as garnish)
Salt & sugar to taste
3-5 tablespoons cooking oil

NOODLES & CONDIMENTS
400g yellow noodles blanched (to remove oil and vinegar)
400g dried rice vermicelli (cooked according to packet instructions)
3-5 stalks kangkong (water convolvulus), blanched
2 handfuls beansprouts, blanched

GARNISH
4 hard-boiled eggs peeled and quartered
2 tablespoons fried shallots (see page 24)
3-5 tablespoons sambal tumis (see page 20)

Blend the dried chillies, shallots and garlic into paste. Heat oil in a wok and fry the spice paste until fragrant. Add prawns and fry for about 5 minutes until the prawn shells are caramelised. Add in sugar and fry for another few minutes.

Add water into the wok and bring it to a boil. Simmer over low heat for at least 15 minutes and remove from heat. When the broth is cooled, fish out the prawns. Shell and dehead the prawns. Set aside the shelled prawns for garnish. Return the shells and head to the broth. Pour the broth into a blender. Liquidise the broth along with the prawn shells. Strain the mixture into a pot.

Add the whole chicken bones and chicken breast to the pot and bring to a boil. Simmer the broth and its contents for at least another 30 minutes on a low heat until the meat is cooked, season to taste with salt. Allow to cool and then shred the chicken breast, set aside for garnish.

To serve place a portion of yellow noodles, rice vermicelli, kangkung and beansprouts in a bowl. Ladle the hot prawn broth over the contents. Garnish with the cooked prawns, shredded chicken, eggs and sprinkling of fried shallots. Serve hot with a spoon of sambal tumis.

PENANG CURRY MEE

SERVES: 4

BROTH PASTE
10 dried red chillies, soaked and deseeded
2 stalks of lemongrass, bruised with the back of a knife
10 shallots
5 garlic cloves
2 tablespoons ground coriander seeds
1 thumb-sized belacan (dried shrimp paste) toasted
Ground white pepper to taste
2-3 tablespoons cooking oil

BROTH
1 litre water
500ml coconut water
100ml thick coconut milk
500ml chicken stock
10 fried beancurd puffs (curry mee is not complete without this)
10 fishballs
250g prawns
Sugar to taste (if you are using coconut water you will not need to add as much sugar)
Salt to taste

GARNISH
400g yellow noodles blanched (to remove oil and vinegar)
400g dried rice vermicelli (cooked according to packet instructions)
150g beansprout, blanched
1 cuttlefish, cleaned and blanched (this is optional as fresh cuttlefish are hard to find and are expensive!)
100g blood cockles, blanched
3-5 long beans cut into 3cm strips, blanched
2-3 sprigs of mint leaves

CURRY MEE SAMBAL
20 dried chillies, soaked and deseeded
2 fresh red chillies
8 shallots
4 garlic cloves
2 tablespoons, dried shrimp soaked
Salt & sugar to taste
3-5 tablespoons cooking oil

Curry mee unlike its counterpart - Hokkien mee - has a coconut milk-based broth. The choice of toppings in a bowl of curry mee differ from region to region in Malaysia; in Penang hawkers usually serve it with a side of coagulated pig's blood. Therefore, Penang-style curry mee is not as thick and has a more aromatic curry broth. The spiciness level of the broth depends on the chilli paste that is served on the side of the bowl. As a Malaysian, I love everything curry based, so my rendition of Penang curry mee is slightly creamier. You can always adjust the quantity of coconut cream you use to suit your preference.

Blend the chillies, lemongrass, shallots, garlic and spice powders into a paste and add some water to loosen the paste. Heat oil in a wok and fry the paste until fragrant. Add coconut milk, coconut water. Add water and chicken stock. Bring the broth to a boil. Season the broth with sugar and salt. Add prawns and fishballs. Let the broth simmer for 20 minutes or so.

Add beancurd puffs and simmer for a few more minutes and continuously stir to prevent the coconut milk from curdling.

CURRY MEE SAMBAL
Blitz the chillies, shallots, garlic cloves and dried shrimp in a food processor into a paste. Heat up some oil in a pan and fry the spice paste until fragrant and the oil separates. Season to taste with salt and sugar. The sambal is ready when it has turned a dark burgundy.

To serve, place some yellow noodles, rice vermicelli, beansprouts and long beans and other preferred garnishes in a bowl. Ladle the hot milky broth over the bowl. Garnish with sprigs of mint leaves and serve with a spoonful of the curry mee sambal.

NASI LEMAK

SERVES: 4

Nasi Lemak is a traditional Malay breakfast staple. Its humble beginnings originated from the kampungs where there are an abundance of coconut trees. To enhance the flavour of the rice, the Malays would cook it with coconut milk. This creaminess gives the dish its name which literally translates as – creamy rice.

A simple, traditional nasi lemak includes coconut rice with hard boiled eggs and fried anchovies in sambal. Over time, it has evolved to include sliced cucumber, roasted peanuts and even pickled vegetables (the latter is a Nyonya favourite). To bring the humble nasi lemak to another level, Malaysians have added even more accompaniments such as sambal sotong, sambal udang and even lobster. Whatever your preference the key to the perfect nasi lemak is in the sambal. When the sambal is done right, everything else falls into place like a beautiful symphony.

Nasi lemak has won the hearts of all Malaysians and has been dubbed Malaysia's national dish. Every time I return from an international trip it's the first thing I crave for. Thank goodness Malaysia Airlines has it on their menu, it's like a welcoming hug on a plate before I touch down on Malaysian soil.

COCONUT RICE
2 cups white rice
200ml of coconut milk
2 cups water
½ red onion, sliced into quarters
1 pandan leaf, tied into a knot
2cm ginger, sliced thinly
Salt to taste

FRIED ANCHOVIES IN SAMBAL TUMIS
1 cup dried anchovies
3-5 heaped tablespoons of sambal tumis (see page 20)
3-5 tablespoons cooking oil

4 hard boiled eggs, cut into halves
1 cucumber, deseeded and sliced
100g peanuts, toasted
Banana leaves (optional)

Let's begin with the coconut rice. Rinse rice thoroughly under the tap then add all ingredients into a pot or rice cooker. Cook till rice is fluffy and fragrant.

Heat up the oil in a wok. Fry the dried anchovies until lightly golden. Set aside to drain the oil.

Using the same oil, fry the homemade sambal tumis. Add the fried anchovies and mix everything together. You can loosen the sambal a little by adding some water.

To serve, scoop the coconut rice into a shallow bowl and tip it over a plate laid with a banana leaf. Serve with anchovy sambal, sliced cucumber, halved hard-boiled egg and peanuts.

COOK'S NOTE
A trick my mother taught me when cooking rice is to rinse the rice a couple of times until the water is about clear. To estimate the amount of water, just immerse your index finger into the rice - the water level should reach the first finger joint. It took me a while to master this because when I was growing up in Malaysia we always had a rice cooker. When I left to study overseas, purchasing a rice cooker was a luxury, so I had no choice but to learn how to cook my rice in a pot (with a little help from my mom's trick!).

NASI KANDAR

If you're in Penang, nasi kandar is a must try. Nasi kandar was originally sold by Indian-Muslim (locally referred to as Mamaks) vendors who carried two large containers of curries and rice on a long pole across their shoulders (the word kandar refers to the pole). At the time, the variety of the dishes was limited because everything had to be hand carried. Today, nasi kandar vendors operate from restaurants and many have evolved into big chains with multiple franchises throughout Malaysia. The most well-known nasi kandar restaurants and brands can still be found in Penang. These are my recipes for my favourite nasi kandar dishes; you don't have to attempt them all in one go though!

Squid Curry

KARI SOTONG

SERVES: 4

SPICE PASTE
5-7 tablespoons onion/shallot paste (see page 24)
2 thumb-sized galangal
1 thumb-sized fresh turmeric
5 candlenuts
2 stalks lemongrass
5 fresh red chillies
5 dried red chillis, soaked
1 thumb-sized belacan (dried shrimp paste), toasted

10-12 squid, cleaned, skinned and gutted
3 tablespoons seafood curry powder mixed with 250ml water
500ml coconut milk
500ml water
2 teaspoons tamarind pulp mixed with 200ml water
3-5 tablespoons cooking oil
Salt & sugar to taste

Blend all the spice paste ingredients in a food processor until a smooth paste. In a deep pot, heat up some oil. Fry the spice paste until aromatic for at least 15-20 minutes, when you can see the oil separate from the paste. Add coconut milk and water. Add squid. Simmer for at least 30-45 minutes until squid are tender and soft. Add the tamarind water. Season with salt and sugar to taste. Stir well. Serve in a deep dish and garnish with white steamed rice.

Fried Chicken in Onion Gravy

AYAM GORENG BAWANG

SERVES: 4

Ayam Goreng Bawang or directly translated means fried chicken with onions. To me, a nasi kandar experience wouldn't be complete without a good fried chicken to soak up the flavourful curry sauces. This elevated version of the fried chicken is a popular dish in most nasi kandar restaurant. It is simple yet packs a lot of flavour.

1 chicken, cut into pieces
2 red onions, sliced thinly
3-5 tablespoons onion/shallot paste (see page 24)
2 tablespoons turmeric powder
1 tablespoon chilli powder
½ teaspoon fennel seed powder
1 teaspoon cumin seed powder
2 tablespoons meat curry powder
1 tablespoon oyster sauce
1 tablespoon chilli sauce
1 tablespoon tomato ketchup
1 cinnamon stick
3 cardamom seeds
2 star anise
3 cloves
2 pandan leaves, tied into a knot
3-5 sprigs curry leaves
Salt & sugar to taste
3-5 tablespoons cooking oil

Fry the sliced onions in oil till golden brown and set aside. Marinate the chicken pieces with salt and turmeric powder for 30 minutes. Deep fry the chicken until golden and crispy on the outside. Set these aside.

Heat up oil in a pan and fry cinnamon stick, star anise, cardamon seeds, cloves, curry leaves, pandan leaves and onion paste until fragrant. Add all the spice powders and stir well. Add a little water to loosen the paste and add chilli sauce, tomato ketchup and oyster sauce. Season the sauce with sugar and salt to taste. Add the fried chicken pieces and fried onion slices. Stir the chicken till fully covered with the onion sauce. Simmer for another 10 – 15 minutes. Serve with steamed white rice.

Captain's Chicken Curry

KARI KAPITAN AYAM

SERVES: 4

---

1 whole chicken, cut into pieces
1 tablespoon turmeric powder
3-5 tablespoons meat curry powder mixed with 250ml water
500ml coconut milk
500ml chicken stock
2 tomatoes, skinned and chopped
1 cinnamon stick
3 cardamom seeds
2 star anise
3 cloves
2 pandan leaves, tied into a knot
3-5 sprigs curry leaves
3-5 tablespoons cooking oil
Salt & sugar to taste

SPICE PASTE
5-7 tablespoons onion/shallot paste (see page 24)
2 thumb-sized galangal
1 thumb-sized fresh turmeric
5 candlenuts
2 stalks of lemongrass
5 fresh red chillies
5 dried red chillies
1 thumb-sized belacan (dried shrimp paste) toasted – optional

GARNISH
Fried shallots (see page 24)

Marinade the chicken pieces with turmeric powder and salt. Heat up oil in a pan and brown the chicken (cook the chicken pieces until ¾ well done). Set these aside.

Blend all the spice paste ingredients in a food processor until a smooth paste. In a deep pot, heat up some oil. Fry cinnamon stick, cardamon seed, star anise, clove, pandan leaf and curry leaf until fragrant. Add the spice paste and meat curry powder mix, fry until aromatic for at least 15-20 minutes and you can see the oil separating from the paste. Add the skinned and chopped tomatoes, cook until soft. Add the chicken pieces and stir well to mix. Add coconut milk and chicken stock. Simmer for at least 30-45 minutes until the chicken is cooked and tender. Season with salt and sugar to taste. Stir well. Serve in a deep dish and garnish with fried shallots.

Spicy Soy Sauce Beef

DAGING MASAK KICAP BEREMPAH

SERVES: 4

Deviating from the usual suspect – curry - daging masak kicap berempah or beef cooked in spicy soy sauce gravy is another staple dish. Don't be deceived by the lack of fiery red in this dish - believe me, it packs some heat.

SPICE PASTE
3-5 tablespoons onion/shallot paste (see page 24)
5 dried chillies, soaked in hot water and deseeded

800g beef, cut into 1 portion serving
2 onions, sliced
2 tomatoes, sliced
1 tablespoon ground coriander powder
1 teaspoon cumin powder
2 tablespoons meat curry powder mixed with 200ml water
5 tablespoons kicap manis (sweet dark soy sauce)
1 cinnamon stick
2 star anise
4 cloves
4 cardamon seeds
1 lemongrass, bruised
2-3 sprigs curry leaves
2 pandan leaves, washed and knotted
2 sprigs coriander leaves, chopped finely for garnish
Salt & sugar to taste
2-3 tablespoons cooking oil

In a food processor, pulverise the spice paste ingredients and set aside. In bowl, mix ground coriander powder, cumin powder and season with salt. Add about 2-3 tablespoons water to form a paste. Add the beef cuts and mix well. Make sure the marinade is evenly distributed and marinate for 15-20 minutes.

Heat up some oil in a pot and fry cinnamon stick, star anise, clove, cardamon seeds, lemongrass, curry leaf and pandan leaf until fragrant. Add the spice paste and continue to fry until aromatic. Add meat curry powder and fry until the oil has slightly separated from the spice paste. Add sliced onions and tomatoes, continue to cook until the tomatoes are pulverised into the gravy. Add the beef cuts. Stir well. Add kicap manis and simmer covered for 30-45 minutes until the beef cuts are soft and tender. Stir occasionally to prevent these sticking to the bottom of the pot. Simmer for another 15 minutes uncovered. Season with sugar and salt to taste. Plate on a deep dish plate and scatter chopped coriander leaves on top. Serve with steamed white rice.

Dhal

KARI DALCA

SERVES: 4

The perfect gravy for steamed white rice and flat breads like roti canai. Kari dalca is also kid-friendly as it is not spicy like most Malaysian dishes!

200g red lentils washed and soaked for 1 hour
800ml water (just remember 1 part lentils to 4 parts water)
2 potatoes medium sized, peeled and cut into bite-sized cubes
2 tomatoes medium sized, skin peeled and roughly chopped
2-3 stalks of curry leaves
5 dried chillies, washed (deseeded if you want less heat)
1 tablespoon mustard seeds
2-3 green chillies, sliced diagonally
2-3 stalks coriander leaves, finely chopped
5 tablespoons onion/shallot paste (see page 24)
1 tablespoon turmeric powder
3 tablespoons ghee
3-5 tablespoons cooking oil
Salt to taste

In a pot bring to a boil enough water to cover the soaked red lentils and potato cubes. Add in half of the onion/shallot paste, all of the chopped tomatoes, sliced green chillies and turmeric powder. Let it simmer for about 20-30 minutes until dhal beans and potatoes have cooked. Continue to simmer over low heat while you make the spice paste.

In a pan, heat up ghee and add mustard seeds. Let the seeds fry a little in the oil and when these start to 'pop' then pick the curry leaves from the stalks and add into the pan. Sauté until fragrant. Add dried chillies and continue to sauté. Then add remaining onion/shallot paste. Let this paste sauté until everything is well mixed, fragrant and caramelised. While the paste is still hot and sizzling, pour this into the simmering red lentil broth. Stir to mix. Continue to simmer until you've achieved the consistency that you like. I prefer it runny enough to be eaten over rice while creamy enough to be picked up with a piece of bread. Season with salt to taste. Then add chopped coriander leaves and stir well. Serve the dhal as an accompaniment to steamed white rice or with roti canai (page 38).

Fish Head Curry

KARI KEPALA IKAN

SERVES: 4

Kari kepala ikan or fish head curry is rich with spices and is a favourite at nasi kandar joints. The perfect accompaniment for steamy, white jasmine rice. You can use any type of fish you want but the typical kari ikan you get from a nasi kandar restaurant is either bawal hitam (black pomfret) or tenggiri (mackerel).

1 large fish head
500g bawal hitam (black pomfret) or tenggiri (mackerel), sliced
1 teaspoon turmeric powder
Salt to taste
5 tablespoons cooking oil

SPICE PASTE
1 ½ teaspoon coriander seeds
1 ½ teaspoon fennel seeds
1 ½ teaspoon cumin seeds
3-5 tablespoons onion/shallot paste (see page 24)
4 tablespoons fish curry powder

CURRY
800ml water
2 teaspoons tamarind pulp mixed with 200ml water
5-8 ladies' fingers
2 tomatoes, cut into wedges
1 large onion, sliced
2 garlic cloves, sliced
1 cinnamon stick
2 star anise
3 cardamon seeds
5 cloves
2 sprigs of curry leaves
125ml coconut milk
Salt & sugar to taste
3-5 tablespoons cooking oil

Marinate the fish with turmeric powder and salt for at least 30 minutes. Heat up the oil in a pan and fry the fish on high heat. Remove the fish from the pan and set aside.

Toast the coriander seeds, fennel seeds and cumin seeds in a dry pan for 1 minute then remove from heat. Blend the toasted seeds with onion/shallot paste. Add curry powder to loosen the paste a little, add 2 tablespoons of water.

Heat up the remaining oil in a wok or pot and fry cinnamon stick, star anise, cardamon seeds, cloves, curry leaves, sliced onions and garlic until fragrant. Add the spice paste and fry until all the ingredients are aromatic and the oil has separated from the spice paste. Add tamarind water (excluding the seeds and pulp). Simmer for at least 10 minutes. Add coconut milk and bring the pot to a boil while stirring occasionally to prevent the coconut milk from curdling. Add ladies' fingers, tomatoes and the fried fish. Season with salt and sugar to taste. The curry is now ready to be served with steamed rice.

Cucumber Salad
KERABU TIMUN

SERVES: 4

2 cucumbers, halved and thinly sliced
2 red onions, thinly sliced
1 fresh green chilli, thinly sliced diagonally
½ cup vinegar
½ cup water
Salt & sugar to taste

Mix all ingredients in a large bowl. Leave to sit for at least 15 minutes before serving.

Onion Salad
KERABU BAWANG

SERVES: 4

3 red onions, thinly sliced
3 tomatoes, quartered and thinly sliced
2 green chillies, sliced
1 teaspoon tamarind pulp mixed with 100ml water
1-2 tablespoons sambal belacan (see page 21)
Salt & sugar to taste

Mix all the ingredients in a large bowl and let it sit for at least 30 minutes before serving.

1. Daging Masak Kicap Berempah (Spicy Soy Sauce Beef)
2. Kerabu Timun (Cucumber Salad)
3. Kari Kapitan Ayam (Captain's Chicken Curry)
4. Kerabu Bawang (Onion Salad)
5. Kari Sotong (Squid Curry)
6. Kari Kepala Ikan (Fish Head Curry)
7. Ayam Goreng Bawang (Fried Chicken in Onion Gravy)

CHAR KUAY TEOW

SERVES: 2

Nothing that gets Penangites all fired up (hotter than a hot wok!) than a discussion about where to find the best char kuay teow.

Char means stir-fry and kuay teow is flat rice noodles. This dish is basically rice noodles fried with Chinese chives, egg, prawns, blood cockles and lap cheong - a Chinese sausage. What gives this fiery noodle dish its flavour are soy sauce and chilli paste. The best tasting char kuay teow is typically fried over a charcoal fire. Somehow this makes the flavour more smoky and sweet. A good char kuay teow will always have the 'wok-hei' aroma which translates as the 'breath of the wok'; a taste acquired only when food is fried at a very high temperature in a seasoned wok (this can only be achieved with an industrial or charcoal stove).

Some hawkers in Penang use big prawns, crab meat and even lobster to make the dish more luxurious. Duck eggs are also used as a substitute for regular chicken eggs and blood cockles were a mainstay of the recipe. The best kuay teow sellers will insist on frying the noodles plate by plate: this way each noodle is well coated with flavour. Just like most of Penang's street food, it is best served on a plate lined with banana leaf for an amazing aroma.

NOODLES & CONDIMENTS
3 garlic cloves, chopped
2 tablespoons chilli paste (see page 20)
8 prawns, shelled
1 chicken breast, cut into thin slices
400g fresh flat rice noodles (kuay teow)
2 tablespoons light soy sauce
1 tablespoon dark soy sauce
2 eggs
2 handfuls beansprouts
3-5 stalks Chinese chives, cut into 2cm strips
100g blood cockles, shelled
Ground white pepper to taste
Salt to taste
2-3 tablespoons cooking oil

Heat oil and fry garlic over a low heat. Turn up the heat and add the chilli paste. Fry until fragrant before adding prawns, blood cockles and chicken slices. Add the kuay teow and stir fry for a few seconds before adding light and dark soy sauce and season with salt.

Make a well in the centre of the kuay teow and add a tablespoon of oil and crack the eggs and season with white pepper. Let the eggs set before scrambling. Stir with the rest of the kuay teow.

Add beansprouts and chives. Stir fry for another 20 seconds before dishing out.

Egg Noodles with Wantan Dumplings
WANTAN MEE

SERVES: 4

Wantan Mee or as the locals call it Tok Tok Mee, is egg noodles served with fried wantan and other toppings such as barbecued pork (char siew), blanched Chinese mustard green (choy sum) chopped spring onions and lard fritters. A small bowl of chicken or pork broth with wantan dumplings are also served as an accompaniment. The secret to a good wantan mee, isn't just in the quality of the egg noodles but also the sauce that clings to the noodles.

WANTAN DUMPLINGS
200g chicken, minced
10 prawns, minced
1 teaspoon cornflour
1 egg
1 teaspoon sesame oil
Ground white pepper to taste
Salt to taste
20-30 wantan wrappers

SEASONING (PER SERVING)
1 teaspoon oyster sauce
1 teaspoon dark soy sauce
Light soy sauce to taste
1 teaspoon sesame oil
1 teaspoon shallot oil (see page 24)

CHICKEN SOUP
800ml chicken stock (see page 23)
Wantan dumplings
Ground white pepper to taste
Salt to taste

GARNISH
800g wantan egg noodles
Barbecued chicken slices (see page 26)
Fried wantan dumplings
3-5 stalks Chinese flower mustard, cut into 5cm strips blanched in boiling water then cold water
2 stalks spring onion, finely chopped
Pickled green chillies (see page 22)

WANTAN DUMPLINGS
In a bowl, mix all the minced meat, minced prawns, cornflour, egg, sesame oil, white pepper and salt. Place a teaspoonful of the mixture in the centre of the wantan wrapper. Pull together the edges of the wrapper to form a bundle and pinch to seal with a little water as a sealing paste.

You can deep fry half of the wantan dumplings and boil the other half in the chicken soup. For the boiled wantan dumplings, boil a pot water and drop the dumplings into the boiling water for 30 seconds. Remove from water and add to the chicken soup before serving.

METHOD
Place the wantan noodles in a perforated ladle and dip into a pot of boiling water for about 30 seconds until the noodles are al dente. Remove and place the cooked noodles into a bowl of cold water for a few seconds. Drain and place it into a bowl.

Add all the seasoning to the cooked noodles and a teaspoon of shallot oil. Toss the noodles well. Place the seasoned noodles on a plate and garnish with sliced barbecued chicken, blanched vegetables and fried wantan dumplings. Serve the noodles with an individual bowl of wantan soup and pickled green chillies.

LAKSA LEMAK

SERVES: 4

Unlike assam laksa (which is often referred to as Penang laksa), laksa lemak can trace its origins back to the Nyonyas. In my recipe, the ingredients are similar to assam laksa with the addition of a few extra ingredients including coconut milk which gives laksa lemak its 'lemak' or creamy flavour.

SPICE PASTE
10 dried chillies, soaked
3-5 tablespoons onion/shallot paste (see page 24)
1 thumb-sized fresh turmeric
2 thumb-sized galangal
3 stalks lemongrass
1 thumb-sized belacan (dried shrimp paste) toasted
3-5 kaffir lime leaves
5 sprigs daun kesom (laksa leaves)
6 candlenuts

FISH BROTH
1 kg ikan kembung (Asian mackerel)
500g fresh prawns
2 bunga kantan (torch ginger flowers), halved
2 teaspoons tamarind pulp mixed with 100ml water
3 asam keping (dried tamarind)
5-8 sprigs daun kesom (laksa leaf)
5 kaffir lime leaves
500ml coconut milk
1 litre water
Salt & sugar to taste

GARNISH
800g fresh laksa noodles
150g beansprouts, blanched
1 cucumber, julienned
2 bunga kantan (torch ginger flower) finely sliced
5 sprigs mint leaves
4 calamansi limes, halved

Blitz all the spice paste ingredients in a food processor until a smooth paste. Boil the fish and prawns in a pot of water until cooked. Remove the fish and prawns from the water and set aside to cool. Set the fish broth aside.

Divide the prawns into two portions – remove the shells from one portion and blitz in a food processor. Save the other portion as a garnish. Once the fish has cooled, debone the fish and set aside for later.

In a new pot, heat up some oil, and fry the spice paste until fragrant. Add bunga kantan, daun kesom, kaffir lime leaves, asam keping, fish and minced prawn. Pour in the fish broth, stir in tamarind juice then add coconut milk. Bring the broth to a boil and simmer at a low heat for 20 – 45 minutes until aromatic. If you find that the broth is too thick, you can add some water. Season to taste with sugar and salt.

To serve, place the fresh laksa noodles in a bowl and garnish with beansprouts, bunga kantan, prawns, cucumber, mint leaves, and calamansi lime. Ladle a good amount of hot broth over the noodles.

Flat Rice Noodle Soup

KUAY TEOW TH'NG

SERVES: 4

Kuay teow th'ng or rice noodles in a clear meat-based soup is as simple as the name implies. Chicken soup is used as the soup base, covering a generous portion of flat rice noodles and topped with garnishes such as fish balls, fish cakes and shredded chicken meat along with spring onions and garlic crisps. It's the Penang version of chicken noodle soup and perfect for breakfast, lunch or when you're feeling under the weather.

CHICKEN SOUP
1 whole chicken carcass, cut into pieces
2 chicken breasts
A generous pot of chicken stock (see page 23)

GARNISH
800g kuay teow (flat rice noodles) blanched in hot water to remove excess oil
15 fish balls
2 chicken breasts, boiled from chicken soup, shredded
3 fried fish cakes, sliced
3 stalks of spring onions, finely sliced
Fried garlic oil (see page 24)
Sliced red chillies or bird's eye chillies

Boil the chicken stock in a large pot and add the chicken carcass and meat. Bring the soup to a boil and lower the heat to simmer for another 30 minutes to 1 hour. Strain the soup into a clean pot. Season the soup to taste with sugar and salt. Add fish balls and bring the soup to a boil again.

Leave the chicken pieces to cool and once cooled, shred the meat. Set aside to use as a garnish. In a serving bowl, place the blanched kuay teow then add about 3-5 fish balls per bowl and slices of fried fish cakes. Ladle the soup over noodles. Top with some shredded chicken and garnish with spring onions and fried garlic oil. Serve with a dipping sauce of sliced red chillies or bird's eye chillies in light soy sauce on the side.

Fried Radish Cake

CHAR KUAY KAK

SERVES: 2

Kuay kak is made by steaming rice flour batter that once cooled forms a firm cake-like thick block. The block is then cut into rough cubes before frying with chilli paste, soy sauce and egg along with preserved radish, garlic, beansprouts and Chinese chives with optional ingredients such as prawns and cockles. The taste and ingredients are somewhat similar in ingredients to the char kuay teow. In this recipe, rice flour cake will be made as the "body" of the dish.

RADISH CAKE
180g radish, shredded
180g rice flour
1 tablespoon tapioca flour
2 garlic cloves, chopped
500ml water
2-3 tablespoons cooking oil
Ground white pepper to taste
Salt & sugar to taste

CHAR KUAY KAK
4 cups radish cake, cut into rough bite-sized cubes
2 garlic cloves, chopped
3 teaspoons preserved radish, roughly chopped - optional
3 tablespoons chilli paste (see page 20)
4 tablespoons light soy sauce
2 tablespoons dark soy sauce
4 eggs
2 handfuls beansprouts
3-5 stalks Chinese chives, cut into 2cm strips
Ground white pepper to taste
2-3 tablespoons cooking oil

RADISH CAKE
Mix rice flour, tapioca flour and water in a bowl until you have a smooth batter. Heat up oil in a pan. Sauté the chopped garlic until fragrant. Add in the shredded radish and stir-fry until the radish is soft and cooked. Add the flour batter into the pan with the cooked radish and mix well. Season with pepper, salt and sugar to taste.

Remove the pan from heat and pour the radish batter into a greased tray to a height of 3-5 cm. Steam the radish batter for 30 minutes in a steamer. Remove from heat and set aside to cool and firm up into a 'cake' texture for a few hours.

CHAR KUAY KAK
Heat up oil in a pan and pan-fry the radish cake cubes over high heat until the cubes are browned. Remove onto a plate and set aside.

In the same pan, heat up more oil and fry the chopped garlic and preserved radish until fragrant. Add chilli paste and fry until the paste is fragrant. Add back the fried cake cubes into the pan and season with light and dark soy sauce. Stir to coat the cubes. Make a well in the middle of the pan and crack in the eggs. Scramble the eggs and mix with the cake cubes. Add beansprouts, Chinese chives and season with ground white pepper. Mix everything well and fry for another minute. Serve while the cakes are hot.

MEE REBUS MAMAK

SERVES: 4

Mee rebus mamak is another Indian Muslim speciality. Typical mamak stalls and eateries will always sell mee rebus together with its brother dish - mee goreng – as both noodle dishes share the same potato gravy and yellow noodles.

GRAVY
500g sweet potatoes or potatoes, peeled and boiled
125g dried shrimps, soaked
1 thumb-sized fresh turmeric
3-5 tablespoons onion/shallot paste (see page 24)
5 dried chillies, soaked
5 fresh chillies
2 tomatoes, diced
2 teaspoons tamarind pulp, diluted in 200ml water
800ml water
Salt & sugar to taste
2-3 tablespoons cooking oil

GARNISH
800g fresh yellow noodles
4 hard boiled eggs
1 large potato, boiled and cut into bite-sized cubes
2 stalks of spring onions, thinly sliced
4 tablespoons fried shallots
2 handfuls beansprout, blanched
2 firm tofu, fried and thinly sliced
8 prawn fritters (see page 36)
4 flour fritters (see page 53)
4 calamansi limes, halved

Blend all the gravy ingredients except for the potatoes, tamarind mix and water, in a food processor. In a pot, heat up oil and pour in the blended spice mix. Add water and potatoes, bring to a boil. Lower the heat and add tamarind water. Simmer for at least 20-30 minutes before adding sugar and salt to taste. Allow the gravy to simmer until it slightly thickens and most of the potatoes have disintegrated.

In a bowl place fresh yellow noodles and garnish with beansprouts, tofu, fritters, spring onions, boiled eggs, boiled potatoes and fried onions. Ladle a generous amount of gravy. Squeeze the lime over the noodles and enjoy.

MEE JAWA

SERVES: 4

Mee jawa may look somewhat similar to mee rebus but has a completely different spice-level and the ingredients are different. Unlike mee rebus, mee jawa's gravy has a meat component to it as beef is usually used to flavour the stock. The gravy is less thick and creamy compared to mee rebus.

SPICE PASTE
3-5 tablespoons onion/shallot paste (see page 24)
5 dried red chillies, soaked
2 tablespoons dried shrimps, soaked
1 stalk of lemongrass

GRAVY
1 litre beef stock
1 large sweet potato
2 teaspoons tamarind pulp mixed with 200ml water
3 tablespoons tomato ketchup
Salt & sugar to taste
2-3 tablespoons cooking oil

GARNISH
800g fresh yellow noodles
100g beansprouts blanched
4 hard boiled eggs
½ lettuce, thinly sliced
2 calamansi limes, halved
2 firm tofu, fried and thinly sliced
8 prawn fritters (see page 36)
Fried shallots (see page 24)

Boil the sweet potatoes until tender. Remove from water and mash them. Set the mashed potatoes aside to cool.

Blend all the spice paste ingredients in a food processor until a smooth paste. Heat up oil in a pot and fry the spice paste until aromatic. Pour in the beef stock into the pot and add the mashed potatoes. Bring the gravy to a boil while stirring occasionally. Lower the heat and simmer for another 15-20 minutes. Add the tomato ketchup, tamarind juice and stir well. Season the gravy with sugar and salt to taste. To serve, place fresh yellow noodles in a deep plate and top with all the garnishing. Ladle a generous amount of gravy over and squeeze in the calamansi lime.

Malay Prawn Noodles

MEE UDANG

SERVES: 4

Mee Udang is the Malay version of prawn mee. It is tomato-based and uses more ingredients from the sea to give it that extra sweetness, the tang of sourness comes from the tomatoes. You can find this at the Malay fishing villages in Teluk Kumbar, where the fresh catch of the day gets served right up from sea to plate. This recipe is inspired by my mom's, and her advice is to make crab stock for an added sweetness that is both tantalizing and indulgent.

CRAB STOCK
2 crabs (medium-sized)
500gm prawns with heads and shells intact
1.5 litres water
Sugar to taste
Salt to taste

GRAVY
10 dried chillies, soaked and seeds removed
3-5 tablespoons onion paste (see page 24)
2 tablespoons dried shrimps, soaked
5 tablespoons tomato ketchup
5 tablespoons chilli sauce
1 teaspoon tomato puree
2-3 stalks choy sum cabbage (Chinese long cabbage) cut into 2cm strips
2 tomatoes, cut into wedges
Salt & sugar to taste

GARNISH
800gm yellow noodles
4 hard boiled eggs, shelled and halved
2 fresh red chillies, thinly sliced diagonally
2 stalks spring onions, thinly sliced diagonally
Fried shallots (see page 24)
4 calamansi limes, halved

In a large pot, heat up some oil. Fry the prawns and crab whole to get some caramelization on the crustaceans and on the pot. Add water and bring it to a boil, simmer for 45 minutes. Season the stock to taste with salt and sugar. Strain the stock and set aside the stock, the cooked prawns and crabs.

In food processor, blend dried chillies, onions, garlic and dried shrimps to a paste. In a wok, heat up a little oil and fry the paste until fragrant. Add tomato ketchup, chilli sauce, tomato puree and mix well. Add in the crab stock ladle by ladle until you get a nice thick soupy consistency (you don't need to use all the stock). Add tomatoes, choy sum and the cooked prawns. Let it simmer for 15-20 minutes. While waiting for the gravy to simmer, you can pick out the crab meat from the shells and set aside for garnishing. Season the gravy to taste with salt and sugar.

To serve, add yellow noodles into a deep dish or bowl. Ladle the gravy over, add some prawns and sprinkle spring onions, red chillies and fried shallots. Garnish with halved boiled egg. Squeeze calamansi lime over the mee udang before eating.

Rice Noodle Salad

KERABU BIHUN

SERVES: 2

Kerabu bihun is a spicy Nyonya rice vermicelli salad. This is a heritage dish that is not so readily available these days but is worth preserving for future generations to rediscover. It's a simple recipe and important to ensure that all the ingredients are fresh (especially the prawns) and of good quality to maximise the taste and flavour.

KERABU DRESSING
2-3 tablespoons sambal belacan (see page 21)
3 tablespoons kerisik (toasted grated coconut)
Juice of 10 calamansi limes
Salt & sugar to taste

GARNISH
300g bihun (rice vermicelli) soaked in water till soft
250g fresh prawns, shelled and cooked
5 shallots, thinly sliced
1 bunga kantan (torch ginger flower) thinly sliced
2-3 sprigs mint leaves, roughly chopped
Fried shallots (see page 24)

In a small bowl, mix all the kerabu dressing ingredients and season with salt and sugar to taste.

In a big mixing bowl, mix together the ingredients while adding the dressing little by little and tasting to season properly. Toss well before serving.

LOH MEE

SERVES: 4

Loh mee is Hainanese in origin and can be translated as gravy noodles. The Hainanese migrants in Malaysia are famous for their culinary skills and their ingenuity in not letting any food go to waste. Loh mee was originally created to salvage leftover sharks fin soup by adding dark soy, noodles and other ingredients to make a wholesome one dish meal (don't worry there is no sharks fin in the modern-day version!).

GRAVY
1 chicken carcass
250g beef bones
500ml chicken stock (see page 23)
1.5 litres water
4 star anise
2 cinnamon sticks
1 teaspoon white peppercorns, crushed
1 teaspoon five-spice powder
3 tablespoons dark soy sauce
3 tablespoons cornflour mixed with water as a thickening solution
1 egg, beaten
Salt to taste

GARNISH
400g fresh yellow noodles, blanched
400g dried rice vermicelli noodles, soaked
2 handfuls beansprouts, blanched
2 chicken breasts, cooked and shredded
4 hard boiled eggs, shelled and halved
Fried shallots (see page 24)
Garlic paste (see page 22)
Garlic chilli sauce (see page 21)

In a large pot boil the chicken carcass, beef bones, star anise, cinnamon sticks, crushed peppercorns and water. Bring the broth to a simmer on low heat for 30 – 45 minutes to reduce. Once reduced, strain the broth to remove bones and spices. Return the clear broth into the pot and add the five-spice powder and dark soy sauce. Season with salt to taste. Bring the broth to a boil again and add the thickening solution (mixture of cornflour and water). Simmer and stir the broth until it thickens. Stir in the beaten egg and turn off heat.

To serve, place some fresh yellow noodles, rice vermicelli noodles and beansprouts in a bowl. Ladle over the thick gravy to cover the noodles. Garnish with shredded chicken, hard-boiled egg and fried shallots. Serve the hot noodles with sides of garlic chilli sauce and garlic paste.

Birthday Noodles

LAM MEE

SERVES: 4

Lam mee also known as Birthday Noodles is usually eaten at birthday celebrations in Nyonya households. This auspicious noodle dish is served in the belief that the long noodles represent longevity. A special touch is the dash of red dye added to the egg to produce a pink omelette (red is considered an auspicious colour for the Chinese). Lam mee is almost always served with sambal belacan to give it a little spicy kick, if not it wouldn't be a Malaysian thing!

BROTH
250g prawn shells and heads
1 litre chicken stock (see page 23)
1 tablespoon soy sauce
1 tablespoon cornflour mixed with water as a thickening agent
Salt to taste
Ground white pepper to taste
2-3 tablespoons cooking oil

GARNISH
800g fresh yellow noodles, blanched
200g prawns, cooked
100g beansprouts, blanched
2 chicken breasts, cooked and shredded
5-8 lettuce leaves, finely sliced
2 stalks of spring onions, finely sliced
Fried shallots (see page 24)
Garlic oil (see page 24)
4 eggs
Red food colouring
Sambal belacan (see page 21)

To make the noodle broth, start by heating up oil in a pot. Fry the prawn shells and heads until fragrant. Add in the chicken stock and bring the broth to a boil, then lower the heat to medium and simmer for another 30 minutes. Season the broth with salt and white pepper to taste. Remove the broth from heat and strain it to remove the prawn shells and heads. Return the broth to the pot on a medium heat. Mix the cornflour with a little water and add it into the broth. Bring the broth to a boil again. Switch off the heat once the broth reaches boiling point.

In a small bowl, crack the eggs and add the food colouring. Beat it with a fork and season the eggs to taste with salt. In a pan heat up some oil and pour in the eggs. Swirl the pan to make a thin omelette. Once cooked remove from pan and set aside to cool. When cool, thinly slice the omelette to use as a garnish.

To serve, place the blanched yellow noodles in a bowl topped with beansprouts, lettuce, prawns, shredded chicken, pink omelette, spring onions and fried shallots. Ladle over the broth to just soak the noodles. Drizzle some garlic oil over and serve with a spoonful of sambal belacan on the side.

PENANG HOKKIEN CHAR

SERVES: 4

Penang Hokkien char as the name suggests is fried noodles cooked in the Hokkien style. Two types of noodles are used in this dish, fresh yellow noodles and bihun (rice vermicelli). The secret to this dish is the gravy used to fry the noodles in. Too dark and it will be a KL-styled Hokkien char, while too light and it will end up being Singapore-style Hokkien char. This is always served with a side of sambal belacan.

BASIC MARINADE FOR CHICKEN
1 tablespoon soy sauce
1 teaspoon sesame oil
1 teaspoon corn flour

400g fresh yellow noodles
400g bihun (rice vermicelli) soaked as per packaging instructions
12 prawns shelled
2 squid, cleaned and sliced thinly
2 chicken breast, sliced thinly
2 stalks choy sum cabbage (Chinese long cabbage), cut into 5cm strips
4 garlic cloves, crushed and minced finely
1 cup of chicken stock (see page 23)
4 tablespoons oyster sauce
4 tablespoons light soy sauce
4 teaspoons dark sweet soy sauce
2 tablespoons fish sauce
2 tablespoons corn flour
200ml water
Salt to taste
2-3 tablespoons cooking oil

GARNISH
4 tablespoons crispy chicken skins (see page 23)
4 tablespoons sambal belacan (see page 21)
2 tablespoons fried shallots (see page 24)

Marinate chicken slices in light soy sauce, sesame oil and corn flour for 15-20 minutes.

Heat up the chicken stock in a small pot. In a pan heat up some oil and add the minced garlic. Fry until aromatic. Add chicken slices, squid and prawns. Do not overcook the seafood. Toss in fresh yellow noodles and soaked bihun. Add oyster sauce, light soy sauce, dark sweet soy sauce and fish sauce. Pour in the chicken stock. In a small bowl mix corn flour with water. Let the noodles simmer in the stock before adding the corn flour mix. Stir well until the gravy thickens. Just before turning off the heat, add choy sum and stir evenly. Remove from heat and serve in a deep plate. Garnish with a spoonful of crispy chicken skins and a side of sambal belacan.

CHAR HOR FUN

SERVES: 4

Hor fun noodles are a type of rice noodle which are thicker than kuay teow (Chinese noodles come in different colours and sizes just like Italian pasta). The hor fun noodles along with vermicelli rice noodles are fried till the soy sauce caramelises before being drenched with an eggy broth that includes prawns and chicken char siew.

600g hor fun (thick rice noodles)
200g bihun (rice vermicelli) soaked in water as per packaging instructions
12 prawns, shelled
2 chicken breasts, thinly sliced
2 pieces of Chinese barbecued chicken (chicken char siew) (see page 26)
4 tablespoons of crispy fried chicken skins (see page 23)
2 stalks of choy sum, cut into 5cm strips
3 eggs
2 garlic cloves, crushed and minced
8 tablespoons light soy sauce
4 tablespoons dark sweet soy sauce
400ml chicken stock (see page 23)
2 tablespoons corn flour
200ml water
Ground white pepper to taste
Salt to taste
2-3 tablespoons cooking oil

Heat up some oil in a pan and add the hor fun noodles and bihun noodles, stir in the light soy sauce and dark sweet soy sauce until well mixed. Charring the noodles will bring out more taste. Remove from pan and set aside.

Add some oil into the pan and fry the minced garlic until aromatic. Add chicken slices, prawns and Chinese barbecued chicken. Then add chicken broth and bring it to a boil. In a small bowl, mix the corn flour with water. Pour the mixture into the broth. Let it simmer to thicken the gravy. Crack in the eggs and stir immediately. Before turning off the heat add choy sum and stir well. Remove the pan from heat.

Serve the soy fried noodles on a deep plate and ladle over some of the gravy. Garnish with a spoonful of crispy chicken skins.

DUCK KUAY CHAP

SERVES: 4

Many of the popular noodle dishes in Penang are soup or gravy-based and kuay chap although well-known, is rather hard to find on the island. The traditional version of kuay chap uses pork broth as its base but I was inspired by a Penang stall that uses duck as the base of their broth. This recipe is ideal for duck lovers and is an excellent alternative to the original.

The 'kuay' part refers to the rice noodle sheets, and 'chap' is the herbal soy sauce-based broth. This is usually served with a tangy chilli sauce and offal (definitely not for the faint of heart!). Instead of using pork belly and offal, I'll be using duck meat and optional duck offal.

1 whole duck (cut into pieces if your pot isn't big enough)
1 cup light soy sauce
1 cup dark soy sauce
1 cinnamon stick
2 star anise
5 cloves
8 garlic cloves, bruised with the back of a knife
3cm fresh ginger, peeled and sliced
1 teaspoon white peppercorns
1 teaspoon black peppercorn
30g rock sugar
2 litres water (enough to cover the duck and other ingredients in the pot)
4 boiled eggs, shelled
2 firm tofu, thickly sliced
800g thick kuay teow (flat rice noodles)
A bunch of coriander leaves, finely chopped
Garlic oil and bits (see page 24)
Garlic chilli sauce (see page 21)

In a large pot, add all spices - cinnamon stick, star anise, cloves - garlic, white and black peppercorns, rock sugar and whole duck. Pour in the light soy sauce and dark soy sauce. Pour in enough water to cover all the ingredients in the pot and bring it to a boil. Turn the heat down and simmer for at least 1 hour. Stir occasionally. Add boiled eggs and firm tofu then simmer for another 1 hour. Stir occasionally. When the duck meat falls off the bone easily, remove the duck, boiled eggs and tofu and set these aside.

In a new pot, pour the dark broth through a sieve to remove all the bits and pieces of spices. Place the broth over a low heat to keep it hot. Once the duck is cool to the touch, shred it and halve the eggs. To serve, place a handful of thick rice noodles in a bowl. Ladle the dark herbal soy sauce broth over and add the shredded duck meat, firm tofu and egg. Sprinkle chopped coriander leaves and add a teaspoonful of garlic oil and bits. Serve with garlic chilli sauce. Alternatively you can eat the duck and broth with steamed white rice (I've also seen it eaten with yam rice or porridge).

HAINANESE CHICKEN RICE

SERVES: 4

What is comfort food for me? Two words. Chicken rice – which is steaming rice cooked in chicken broth served with a portion of poached chicken, with garlic chilli sauce and ginger spring onion oil.

Hainanese chicken rice did not actually originate from the Hainan region in China but rather from the Hainanese people who migrated to Malaysia and Singapore. It's one of those simple, super delicious dishes that is loved by kids and adults and is suitable for all occasions. As I'm part Hainanese myself, on my father's side, this dish has a special place in my heart. If you eat this on the streets of Penang, it's very likely that the chicken stock is loaded with MSG to achieve that savoury flavour we're all addicted to; my recipe is without the MSG.

POACHED CHICKEN
1 whole chicken, washed
1 whole chicken carcass, washed
3 thumb-sized ginger, roughly sliced
3 stalks of spring onions, cut into half (separate the white section from the green section)
1-2 tablespoons sesame oil
1 cucumber, sliced or cut into strips to use as garnish
2 litres water
Salt to taste

RICE
1-2 teaspoons garlic paste (see page 22)
Chicken fat and skin
2 cups of rice, washed
3 ½ cups chicken stock (from the poached chicken)
1 pandan leaf washed and knotted
Salt to taste
2-3 tablespoons cooking oil

POACHING THE CHICKEN
Cut the chicken fat around the neck with a pair of scissors and save for the rice.

Sprinkle a generous amount of salt over the chicken and thoroughly massage the salt into the chicken and inside the cavity. In large pot add the green sections of spring onion and roughly sliced ginger. Season the water with a little salt. Poach the whole chicken (very gently) and chicken carcass on a low heat for 45 minutes to 1 hour until the chicken is thoroughly cooked. Take care not to tear the chicken skin from the poached chicken and save the chicken stock for the rice and sauce.

PREPARING THE RICE
In a pot, heat up some oil. Fry the chicken fat and skin gently over a medium heat to render out the fat into the oil. Once the fat and skin are golden, remove these from the oil. Add garlic paste and fry until fragrant then add rice and stir well to coat each grain of rice with oil. Add chicken broth and knotted pandan leaf and rice, simmer on low heat until all the water is absorbed. Cover with a lid to cook the rice until it's fluffy and glossy. Alternatively, you can cook your rice to perfection in a rice cooker.

GARLIC CHILLI SAUCE
3 red chillies (deseeded if you want less heat)
2 thumb-sized ginger, peeled and roughly diced
3-5 garlic cloves
2 tablespoons white vinegar
1-2 ladles of chicken broth from the poached chicken
Salt & sugar to taste

GINGER SPRING ONION OIL
5 stalks of spring onion
5 thumb-sized ginger, peeled and roughly diced
Salt to taste
2 tablespoons cooking oil (use a neutral tasting vegetable oil)

LIGHT SOY SAUCE DRESSING FOR THE CHICKEN
3-5 ladles chicken broth
3-5 tablespoons soy sauce
1-2 tablespoons of sesame oil

In a bowl mix chicken broth with soy sauce and sesame oil. Stir well.

GARLIC CHILLI SAUCE
In a food processor, blitz the red chillies, ginger, garlic with salt and sugar. Transfer into a bowl and add white vinegar. Add a few tablespoons of warm chicken broth. Mix well and season to taste, the sauce should be more sweet than spicy.

GINGER SPRING ONION OIL
Roughly chop the spring onion and blitz together with the ginger and a sprinkling of salt, into a paste. Transfer the paste into a bowl.

In a small pot, heat up the oil on a low heat. Once the oil is heated, pour the hot oil into the ginger spring onion paste. Stir well and season with salt to taste.

Finally! We're almost at the eating part! Gently remove the whole chicken from the broth and rub the entire chicken with sesame oil to give it a glossy sheen. Cut it into serving portions without tearing the skin.

Plate the chicken with a serving of steamed rice and garnish with cucumber slices. Drizzle the light soy sauce dressing over the chicken and serve together with a bowl of the chicken broth, chilli garlic sauce and ginger spring onion oil.

> **COOK'S NOTE**
> *The key to this dish is all about the gentle poaching of the chicken so as not to damage the chicken skin (which is a distinctive feature of Hainanese chicken rice). The chicken broth unites all the parts of this dish harmoniously, so if your chicken broth is sublime, everything else will fall into place. If you have the time and energy you can use a mortar and pestle to grind the sauce ingredients the traditional way.*

HAINANESE CHICKEN CHOP

SERVES: 4

Chicken chop is another Hainan-inspired dish that did not originate from Hainan, China but rather developed from Hainanese migrants living in Malaysia and Singapore. This is their take on western cuisine and was one of my childhood favourites.

I personally prefer the version that uses canned peas instead of frozen peas, there's just something about the difference in texture and taste, and I find that canned peas are meatier and softer, just the way I like it.

POTATO WEDGES
4 russet potatoes, skin left on but washed thoroughly
Cooking oil for deep frying
Salt to taste
Ground black pepper to taste

CHICKEN CHOPS
4 chicken drumsticks, bones removed, skin left on
2 eggs
1 cup flour
1 tablespoon cornflour
1 teaspoon five spice powder
1 teaspoon garlic powder
Ground white pepper to taste
Salt to taste
Cooking oil for deep frying

TOMATO SAUCE
2 tomatoes medium to large sized, cut into wedges
2 white onions, cut into wedges
1 can of peas (or 1 cup of frozen green peas)

Cut the potatoes into wedges of equal size. Using a kitchen towel, dry the potatoes thoroughly. In a pan heat up enough oil to deep fry the potatoes. Gently put the potatoes into the hot oil and fry until light golden brown. Remove from oil and drain excess oil on a paper towel. Fry the potatoes a second time until golden brown and the inside is soft and fluffy. Remove from oil and drain excess oil on a paper towel. Transfer into a bowl and season with salt and ground black pepper. Toss the wedges to evenly coat the seasoning.

Tenderise and flatten the chicken legs. In a bowl crack in the eggs and beat. On a plate mix the flour, cornflour, five spice powder, garlic powder and season with salt and ground white pepper. Dip the chicken legs one at a time into the beaten eggs, then coat the legs with the flour mix, be sure to cover the entire chicken leg.

In a pot or pan, heat up enough oil to deep fry the chicken legs. Make sure the oil is hot before putting the chicken leg in. Do not overcrowd your pot or pan. Fry the chicken legs until golden brown and make sure that both sides are evenly cooked (check that the insides are cooked properly). Remove from the pan and drain excess oil on a paper towel.

3 tablespoons tomato ketchup
2 tablespoons Worcestershire sauce
3 tablespoons HP brown sauce
200ml water (to loosen the sauce)
Salt & sugar to taste
2-3 tablespoons cooking oil

In a pan, heat up a little oil and sauté the onions. Then add tomatoes and sauté until soft. Add tomato ketchup, Worcestershire sauce and brown sauce. Loosen the sauce with a little water. Season with sugar and salt if needed. Finally add the canned peas. Continue to simmer until the peas are heated through. The sauce should be thick but runny enough to be drizzled over the chicken. When the right consistency is achieved, turn off heat.

Serve each chicken chop on a plate with wedges and ladle the warm sauce over the chicken.

DESSERTS & DRINKS

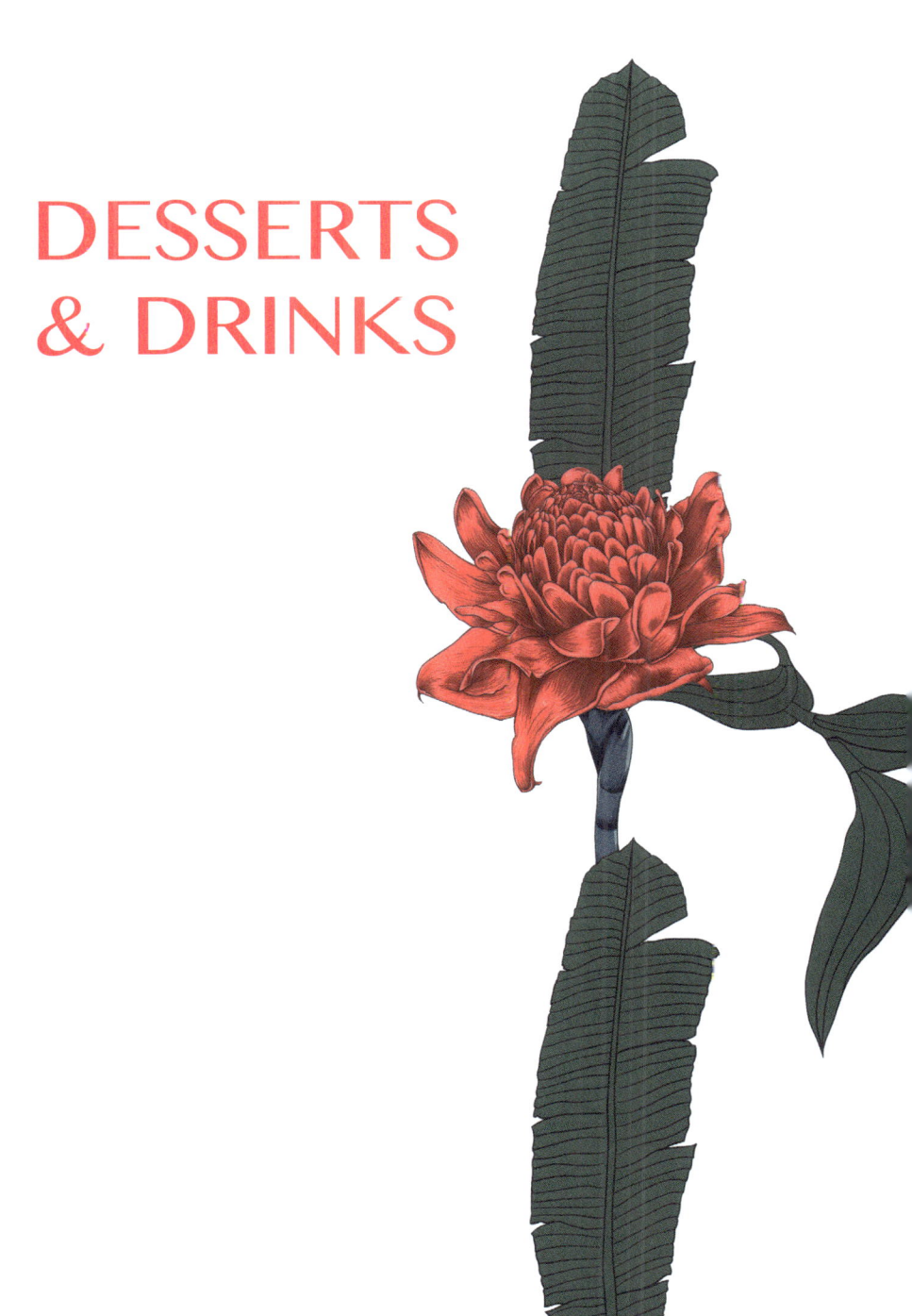

SOY MILK

SERVES: 4

400g soy beans, soaked in water overnight
2 litres water
1 pandan leaf

GULA MELAKA SYRUP
See page 135

Drain the soy beans. Blend the beans with 2 litres of water in a blender. Strain the bean and water mixture through a muslin cloth into a pot. Add the pandan leaf and bring to a gentle boil the milk on a medium heat while stirring continuously for 20 minutes.

Remove the pandan leaf and skim the foam off the surface of the milk. Leave the milk to cool and refrigerate before consuming or if you prefer you can serve it while it's hot. Add sugar syrup to sweeten.

Soy Milk Pudding
TAU FOO FAH

SERVES: 4

1 litre fresh soy milk (see recipe above. Please take note that store-bought soy milk will not give you good results!)
2 pandan leaves tied into a knot
½ teaspoon GDL powder (or gypsum powder which is a soy milk coagulant and is available at baking supply shops)
2 tablespoons cornflour mixed with 200ml water

Add the soy milk and pandan leaf to a pot and boil over a medium heat while stirring continuously. Turn the heat off once the milk comes to a boil. Remove the pandan leaf and skim the foam off the milk's surface. Mix the GDL powder and cornflour with the soy milk then pour the mixture into a thermos pot or rice cooker (don't turn the cooker on!).

Wrap the thermos pot cover with a dry muslin cloth. The cloth helps to absorb the steam so that it will not drip on your tau foo fah. Allow the tofu to set for at least 2 hours (do not remove the cover before then, patience is key). After 2 hours, remove the lid and remove any foam that has accumulated on the surface of the tofu. Using a large flat spoon or ladle, scoop the tofu into small bowls, serve while it's hot with gula Melaka syrup (see page 135).

Slow-Cooked Pancake/Apom Balik

BAN CHANG KUIH

SERVES: 4

This is a thick fluffy Chinese pancake filled with crushed peanuts, crunchy brown sugar and creamy sweetcorn. Each pancake is slow-cooked for around 5-10 minutes to achieve a crispy exterior and soft fluffy middle. I have to say that making these at home really tested my skills! It took a lot of tries to get the pancake right so don't be too hard on yourself if your version doesn't look like the ones you buy at a hawker stall. It's also worth noting that hawkers have spent years perfecting their art (if not generations) and have special pancake pans for their ban chang kuih.

½ cup rice flour
1 ½ cups wheat flour
1 ½ teaspoons bicarbonate of soda
¾ cup brown sugar
180ml coconut milk
300ml water
3 eggs
1 cup peanuts, toasted and crushed
1 cup brown sugar
5 tablespoons butter
1 can of creamy sweetcorn
Salt to taste
Cooking oil or butter to grease the pan

Mix rice flour, plain flour, bicarbonate of soda, sugar and salt in a bowl. Add eggs, coconut milk and water. Whisk the batter until smooth. Cover the bowl with cling film and leave to rest for at least 30 minutes or overnight in the fridge. From my experience, leaving the batter overnight in the fridge yields the best results.

In a bowl mix the toasted crushed peanuts with brown sugar. Lightly grease a non-stick pan over a medium heat. Once the pan is warm, add a ladle full of batter. Aim to make the pancake about 1cm thick. Cover the pan and let the pancake cook for 3 minutes. Once the pancake surface starts to bubble it should look like a beehive, with lots of bubble holes, uncover the pan and sprinkle the crushed peanuts and sugar mix evenly all over the pancake. Cover the pan to continue cooking for another 3 minutes until the edges of the pancake are brown and crispy. Add a dollop of butter and let it melt then add a heaped tablespoon of creamy sweetcorn to the pancake. Fold the pancake into half while it's hot and in the pan, remove from pan and serve while warm and crispy.

Sweet Herbal Dessert Soup

LENG CHEE KANG

SERVES: 4

Leng chee kang is a clear sweet dessert soup originally made with four ingredients - dried longan, gingko nuts, lotus seeds and white fungus. If you want to modify or upgrade your version, you can also add juicy red dates, Chinese barley, candied winter melon, getah anggur, agar-agar, sweet potato cubes and goji berries. Leng chee kang can be served hot or cold and is especially refreshing on a hot day. My paternal grandmother used to make this for us during Chinese New Year as something refreshing and sweet to usher in the new year.

¼ cup dried longans
¼ cup dried lotus seeds
¼ cup gingko nuts
3 tablespoons Chinese barley
3 large blossoms white fungus
¼ cup dried winter melon
3 pandan leaves tied into a knot
Rock sugar to taste
2 litres water

Soak the gingko nuts overnight and remove the bitter core with a toothpick. Soak the barley and white fungus for at least 2 hours.

Fill a pot with water and boil the barley and gingko nuts first for at least 30 minutes. Add the soaked white fungus and boil for another 30 minutes. Add pandan leaves, dried longan, dried winter melon, lotus seeds and rock sugar. Simmer for another 30 minutes. Serve hot or chilled.

PEGAGA JUICE

SERVES: 4

This green juice is great for dispelling body heat during Penang's all-year hot weather. In Hokkien it is known as cheh chao and jus pegaga in Malay.

200g daun pegaga (Asian Pennywort leaves)
3 pandan leaves
1 litre water
200g gula Melaka (palm sugar)
250ml water
A pinch of salt

Wash the Asian Pennywort and pandan and cut these into small rough pieces. Blitz the leaves with water in an electric blender. Sieve the blended juice.

Chop or shave the palm sugar with a knife. In a saucepan, simmer the sugar shavings with some water to make a sweet syrup. Serve the juice warm or chilled and add the palm sugar syrup to sweeten and a pinch of salt to balance the taste.

Pulled Tea
TEH TARIK

SERVES: 2

As the name implies, pulled tea involves the transfer of tea from one large mug to another to incorporate air into the tea which creates a lovely frothy foam. If you were to order a cup of teh tarik in a mamak shop, the teabags used would be a robust heavy duty tea brand, which is not a bad thing. The darker and more intense the tea, the better the flavour. Now let's get pullin'!

2 black tea bags (it's up to you how strong you like your tea!)
500ml hot water
2-3 tablespoons of condensed milk

In a large mug, steep the teabag(s) for 3-4 minutes until dark and rich. Remove the bag(s) and add in condensed milk. Get another large mug ready and slowly pour the tea from one mug to the other, with each pour higher than the one before. It's best to do this over the kitchen sink so that you don't make too much of a mess! If you prefer more froth, continue to 'pull' the tea.

Shaved Ice with Red Beans, Sugar Syrup and Evaporated Milk

AIS KACANG

SERVES: 4

Ais kacang is eaten and loved throughout Malaysia and in Penang it is usually served with red beans, grass jelly and ground peanuts topped off with a scoop of ice-cream!

RED BEANS
150g dried red kidney beans
1 pandan leaf
500ml water
Sugar to taste

GULA MELAKA SYRUP
200g gula Melaka (palm sugar)
1 pandan leaf
250ml water

TOPPINGS
1 can sweet corn
1 cup cincau jelly (grass jelly block) cut into little bite-sized cubes
1 cup tapioca balls (in red or green)
1 cup attap chee (whole palm fruits)
100g peanuts, toasted and roughly crushed
Shaved ice
1 can of evaporated milk
300ml rose syrup (see page 149)
Vanilla ice cream

RED BEANS
Wash and soak the dried red beans overnight. Rinse the beans before putting them in a pot with water and the knotted pandan leaf. Bring it to a boil and simmer over medium heat while occasionally stirring the beans. Simmer until the beans are tender then add sugar. Once cooked leave aside to cool.

GULA MELAKA SYRUP
To make gula Melaka syrup, shave gula Melaka to dust. In a small pot, add the water and shaved gula Melaka. Bring the syrup to a boil and once it has achieved a sticky consistency, let it cool (it can be stored in an air-tight jar in the fridge).

ASSEMBLING THE AIS KACANG
To make shaved ice, blend ice cubes in a powerful blender. The amount of ice needed would depend on the size of your bowl, as a general rule, be generous and aim for a 'mountain' of snow!

Place a generous serving of red beans, sweet corn, grass jelly cubes, tapioca balls and attap chee fruits in a bowl. Add the shaved ice and drizzle red rose syrup, evaporated milk and the gula Melaka syrup all over the shaved ice. Sprinkle a generous amount of toasted crushed peanuts on top and finish it with a scoop of vanilla ice cream. Dig in before it melts!

Shaved Ice with Coconut Milk, Red Beans and Pandan Jelly Noodles

CENDOL

SERVES: 4

A bowl of cool silky coconut milk drenched over shaved ice, sticky sweet red beans and green chewy pandan jelly noodles is the perfect thirst-quencher on a hot day. My favourite stall is the original Penang Road cendol stall which is now a national icon run by the third generation.

RED BEANS
150g dried red kidney beans
1 pandan leaf
500ml water
Sugar to taste

GULA MELAKA SYRUP
See page 135

PANDAN JELLY NOODLES
20 pandan leaves (the more you use the more aromatic the jelly will be)
500ml water
150g mung bean flour (or tapioca flour)
1 tablespoon alkaline water
Salt & sugar to taste

SHAVED ICE
500ml coconut milk (if you can't get your hands on fresh coconut milk, dilute some coconut cream with warm water and add a little salt to taste)
Salt to taste

RED BEANS
Wash the red beans and soak overnight. Add the beans and water to a pot and bring to a boil, add the brown sugar and stir. Cook the beans until they are tender, the sugar has dissolved and the water has evaporated. Set aside to cool.

PANDAN JELLY NOODLES
Cut the pandan leaves into small pieces. Put the pieces in a blender and add water. Blitz until smooth. Sieve the pandan mixture through a fine strainer. In a pot on a medium heat, pour the pandan water and add the flour, and alkaline water. Mix well. Add salt and sugar while continuing to stir until the mixture becomes a sticky paste. Prepare a bowl of ice water with ice cubes. Scoop the jelly mixture into a potato ricer and squeeze out the green little noodles into the bowl of ice water. Continue to squeeze the jelly through the potato ricer until the jelly mixture is finished. Remove the jelly noodles from the ice water and set aside in a bowl.

ASSEMBLING THE CENDOL
To make shaved ice, blend ice cubes in a powerful blender. The amount of ice needed would depend on the size of your bowl, as a general rule, be generous and aim for a 'mountain' of snow! To assemble the cendol, place the shaved ice, pandan jelly noodles followed by red beans in a bowl. Pour on the coconut milk and top with gula Melaka syrup.

Peanut Covered Sticky Glutinous Rice Doughballs

MUAR CHEE

SERVES: 2

Muar chee is a street food snack that packs a punch. I love its chewy texture, peanuty goodness and the aroma of the shallot oil. I would trade a bag of potato chips for a small serving of muar chee, any day, any time!

PEANUT COATING
100g peanuts, toasted
50g sugar (or brown sugar)
20g sesame seeds, toasted

STICKY DOUGH
180g glutinous rice flour
200ml water
Shallot oil (see page 24)

Start by making the peanut sesame dust. In a small pan, toast the peanuts until fragrant and slightly browned. Remove from heat and let these cool. Transfer the peanuts into a food processor along with toasted sesame seeds and blitz till super fine. On a clean plate, scatter your ground peanuts, sesame seeds, sugar and mix well. Set aside while you make the sticky dough.

In a bowl, mix the glutinous rice flour with water, add a tablespoon of shallot oil and mix well.

In a heated pan add shallot oil and swirl it to cover the pan. Pour the flour mixture over low heat. Use a pair of chopsticks and stir the mixture until it forms a dough. Tear and fold the dough as you go. Once the colour of the dough is even throughout and the dough is sticky in consistency with a shiny, glossy coat, it is done. This should take about 15-20 minutes. Always watch the heat and keep it low so as to not burn the dough. Remove the dough and pan from the heat and let it cool.

Oil a pair scissors and cut the dough into bite-sized pieces. Mix well in the peanut sesame dust and serve while warm.

Banana Fritters

PISANG GORENG

SERVES: 4

Although typically sold by street vendors as an afternoon snack you can now find fritters served in restaurants and jazzed up with ice cream and syrup. Growing up in my grandparents' house, we would either have banana fritters or cucur udang (see page 36) as a teatime treat with black tea or coffee. Yum!

The secret to great banana fritters lies in choosing the right banana and the batter. The number one banana to use is 'pisang raja'. But if you can't find these, any local banana will do. Do not be tempted to use cavendish bananas as these are not cooking bananas and are best eaten raw.

6 bananas, peeled and halved lengthwise
½ cup plain flour
¼ cup corn flour
1 tablespoon rice flour
½ teaspoon baking powder
100ml cold sparkling water (optional) or cold still water
Salt to taste
Cooking oil for deep frying

In a medium sized bowl, mix all the flour and salt. Slowly add the cold water and mix well. You are aiming for a smooth consistency and make sure there are no lumps. If the batter is too thick, add more water but make sure that the batter is not too runny. Dip your halved bananas in the batter one by one, so that they don't stick to each other. Heat up your oil in a wok or pan that's deep enough for deep frying, at a temperature of 180C. Gently slide the batter covered banana into the oil once it's hot. Deep fry until golden brown while flipping on each side. Do not overcrowd the oil. Once these are ready remove the fritters from the oil onto some paper towels to absorb excess oil. Serve while hot with coffee or tea or if you have a sweet tooth, with a scoop of ice cream.

NUTMEG JUICE

SERVES: 4

Nutmeg is a famous commodity grown in Penang and there was a time when it was more valuable than gold. Here in Penang it is not only used as a spice but also as a thirst quencher. You can buy ready-made nutmeg cordial in the supermarkets these days but why not make it yourself without the added preservatives. Alternatively you can make fresh nutmeg juice by blending fresh ripe nutmegs in a juicer.

500g fresh nutmegs, cleaned, halved, deseeded
1 litre water
250g sugar

Put all the ingredients in a pot and bring to a boil. Simmer on medium to low heat for at least 2 – 4 hours. You will only need to stir it occasionally. Strain the juice. Pour back the strained juice into a pot and simmer for another 2 – 4 hours until a thick syrup is formed. Set aside to cool and store in a sterilised glass jar or bottle. The syrup will keep up to a month or longer if stored in the fridge. To serve add water to the cordial and add ice, you can also enjoy it warm.

AMBRA JUICE

SERVES: 2

Ambra is a sour, salty, sweet concoction packed with Vitamin C and perfect for the heat.

10 ambra fruits (buah kendondong) cleaned, skinned and deseeded, cut into small pieces
4 dried sour plums (this is important not only for sourness but also a hint of saltiness)
500ml water
Sugar to taste
Ice cubes

In a blender blitz the ambra fruits, sugar and water until smooth. Sieve the mixture through a fine sieve. Alternatively, you can put the ambra fruits through a juicer and later add water and sugar. Pour over ice cubes and add 2 pieces of dried sour plums per glass.

BUBUR CHA CHA

SERVES: 4

Bubur cha cha is an infusion of creamy coconut broth with fibrous root vegetables, sweet gula Melaka, sago pearls and tapioca jellies. It is usually served warm, but can also be served chilled.

TAPIOCA JELLY
80g tapioca flour
50ml hot water
Food colouring (your choice of colour)

BUBUR
½ yam, peeled and cut into bite-sized cubes
2 sweet potatoes (choose as many colours as you can yellow, orange, purple) peeled and cut into bite-sized cubes
½ cup gula Melaka (palm sugar or brown sugar)
200ml coconut milk
200ml water
2-3 tablespoons sago pearls
2 pandan leaves, washed and knotted

In a mixing bowl, add tapioca flour and hot water and mix well. Add food colouring and continue to knead the dough until the colour is evenly distributed. Divide the dough into bite-sizes and roll into little balls (or any other shape you prefer!). Dust a little tapioca flour onto the balls if they are too sticky to handle.

In a pot, bring some water to a boil and gently drop the tapioca balls into the boiling water. Let these cook for 15 minutes or until the balls float on the surface. Once these are cooked, put these into a bowl of cold water to stop the balls from sticking to each other and stop the cooking process.

Boil or steam the yam and sweet potato cubes. Both will have different cooking time therefore it's best to cook these separately. Once cooked, set these aside.

In a small pot, bring some water to a boil. Add sago and let it simmer over medium heat for about 15 minutes. When the sago is cooked it will become translucent. Transfer the sago with a fine sieve into a bowl of cold water and set aside.

In another pot, bring some water to a boil and add *gula Melaka* and knotted pandan leaves, stir gently until the sugar is dissolved. Turn the heat to low and gently add coconut milk with a pinch of salt to taste. Once you've achieved a creamy broth consistency add cooked yam and sweet potato cubes, tapioca jellies and sago. Let the mixture simmer for 10-15 minutes while stirring occasionally. To serve, ladle into individual bowl and serve warm. Alternatively, you can store the *bubur* in the fridge for a couple of hours and serve cold.

BUBUR PULUT HITAM

SERVES: 4

Bubur in Malay means porridge. Bubur pulut hitam can be literally translated as black glutinous rice porridge. This is a traditional Malay dessert served warm or at room temperature and is served with fresh coconut cream. The recipe is simple with humble ingredients yet it has a rich and luxurious taste and consistency.

Some street vendors selling bubur will add black and white glutinous rice to their recipe but my recipe only uses black glutinous rice. Unlike other Malaysian desserts, the coconut cream is not added to the porridge while it's being cooked but rather just before serving. A pinch of salt is added to the coconut cream to help keep the coconut fresh and from turning sour quickly; in my opinion the hint of salt brings out the sweetness of the bubur.

COCONUT CREAM
100ml fresh thick coconut milk
A pinch of salt to taste

BUBUR
150g black glutinous rice
1 litre water
50g sugar (white or brown)
2 pandan leaves, washed and knotted

In a bowl mix the coconut milk with a pinch of salt. Keep it in the refrigerator while you make the bubur.

Wash the black glutinous rice. In a pot, boil black glutinous rice in water with knotted pandan leaves. Bring it to a boil then lower the heat and let it simmer for 45 minutes to 1 hour. Add sugar and stir to mix. Bring the porridge to a boil again until the black glutinous rice grains are completely cooked and have formed a thick porridge. To serve, ladle the porridge into individual bowls and just before eating, spoon a generous amount of fresh coconut cream on top.

AIS TINGKAP

SERVES: 2

Found only in Penang, ais tingkap is a soda drink made of rose syrup, coconut water and everything sweet. Ais tingkap or window sherbet began when a drinks vendor decided to start selling his concoctions through the window of his shop.

ROSE SYRUP
5 cloves
1 cinnamon stick
2 star anise
3 cardamom pods
1 ½ cup white sugar
1 pandan leaf, washed and knotted
500ml water
Red food colouring

Ice cubes for two glasses
600ml coconut water (fresh if possible)
6 scoops of coconut meat
4 tablespoons of biji selasih (basil seeds) soaked in water for at least 30 minutes or left overnight in the fridge
4 tablespoons of getah anggur (almond gum) soaked in water for at least 2-3 hours or left overnight in the fridge (optional)
6 tablespoons of rose syrup

In a pot bring all the ingredients (except for the red food colouring) to a boil. Turn down the heat to medium and simmer until the syrup thickens. Add red food colouring and stir well. Remove from heat and let the syrup cool completely before removing the spices and pandan leaves. Transfer to a sterilised glass jar or bottle and store in the fridge (up to a month).

Fill one third of a large glass with ice cubes. Spoon in the getah anggur and biji selasih. Add rose syrup (to suit your preference). Pour in coconut water and stir well. Scoop out some coconut flesh and add to the glass.

INDEX

Ais kacang 134-135
Ais tingkap 148-149
Alkaline water (kansui water) 18, 47, 136
Ambra juice 143
Assam keping/assam gelugor (dried tamarind slices) 12
Ayam goreng bawang 81, 89

Ban chang kuih (apom balik) 9, 128-129
Banana leaf 14, 44, 55, 78, 91
Belacan (prawn paste) 15, 20-22, 48, 51, 55, 61, 63, 71, 77, 80, 83, 87, 94, 106, 110, 113
Blood cockles 17, 77, 91
Buah keras (candlenut) 12, 55
Bubur cha cha 144-145
Bubur pulut hitam 146-147
Bunga kantan (torch ginger flower) 11, 71, 94, 106

Cendol 136-137
Chai kuih (steamed vegetable dumplings) 58-59
Char hor fun 26, 114-115
Char kuay kak (fried radish cake) 14, 98-99
Char kuay teow 6, 12, 14, 17, 90-91, 98
Chee cheong fun 15, 24, 46-47
Cheh chao 132
Cheh hu (Chinese pasembur) 52-53
Chicken char siew (barbecued chicken) 26, 114
Chicken noodle soup 97
Chicken stock 23, 29, 77, 83, 93, 97, 109-110, 113-114, 118
Cili merah (fresh red chillies) 14, 20-21, 51, 55, 62-63, 71, 77, 80, 83, 97, 102, 105, 119
Chilli paste 20-21, 53, 72, 77, 91, 98
Chilli sauce 20-21, 29, 31-32, 37, 44, 47-48, 53, 56, 59, 61, 67, 72, 81, 105, 109, 117-119
Chinese fermented red beancurd 18, 26
Crispy fried chicken skin 23
Crispy fried shallots 23-24, 47
Cucur udang (prawn fritters) 12, 29, 36-37, 51, 53, 101-102, 140
Curry mee 15, 17, 76-77
Curry mee sambal 77
Cuttlefish 15, 25, 53, 61, 63, 77

Daging masak kicap berempah 84, 89
Daun kesom (laksa leaves) 71, 94
Daun kuchai (chinese chives) 12, 44, 59, 91, 98
Daun pandan (pandan leaves) 12, 35, 78, 81, 83-84, 118, 127, 131-132, 135-136, 145-146, 149
Dried beancurd skin 17, 29
Dried longan 14, 131
Duck kuay chap 116-117

Fish balls 17, 97
Fish cakes 17, 51, 97
Flour fritters 51, 53, 101

Garlic bits 23-24
Garlic chilli sauce 20-21, 44, 47, 109, 117-118
Garlic oil 24, 59, 97, 110, 117
Garlic paste 22, 24, 26, 109, 118
GDL powder 14, 127
Ginger spring onion oil 65, 118-119
Gula melaka (palm sugar) 15, 35, 61, 63, 132, 135, 145

Hae ko (black prawn paste) 15, 47-48, 61, 71
Hainanese chicken chop 121-122
Hainanese chicken rice 118-120
Halia (ginger) 11-12, 14, 24, 63, 65, 71, 78, 117-119
Half-boiled eggs 35

Kacang panjang (long green beans) 14, 32, 77
Kari dalca 41, 85
Kari kapitan ayam 82-83, 89
Kari kepala ikan 86, 89
Kari sotong (squid curry) 89-90
Kaya 34-35
Kerabu bawang (onion salad) 87-88
Kerabu bihun 106-107
Kerabu timun (cucumber salad) 87-88
Kerisik 17, 106
Kicap manis (sweet dark soy sauce) 18, 26, 29, 61, 72, 84, 91, 93, 98, 109, 117
Kuay teow th'ng 21, 96-97
Kunyit (turmeric) 12, 37, 43, 55, 80-81, 83, 85-86, 94, 101

Laksa lemak 94-95
Lam mee (birthday noodles) 110-111
Leng chee kang 130-131
Lengkuas (galangal) 11, 14, 55, 63, 71, 30, 83, 94
Light soy sauce dressing 119
Limau kasturi (calamansi lime) 11, 48, 72, 94, 102, 105
Loh mee 108-109
Lok lok (skewers hotpot) 9, 62-64
Lor bak 29

Mee goreng mamak 72-73
Mee jawa 102-103
Mee rebus mamak 100-101
Mee udang (malay prawn noodles) 104-105
Muar chee 24, 138-139
Murtabak 22, 42-43

Nasi kandar 80-81, 86
Nasi lemak 7, 14, 25, 78-79
Nutmeg juice 142

Oh chien 6, 14, 44
Or kuih (taro/yam cake) 56-57
Otak-otak 54-55

Pasembur 17, 37, 50-53
Pegaga juice 132
Penang assam laksa 10, 70-71, 94
Penang hokkien char 112-113
Penang hokkien mee (chinese prawn noodles) 75, 76-77
Penang rojak 48-49
Pickled green chillies 22, 93
Pink pickled onions 22, 43
Pisang goreng 140-141
Poached chicken 118-119
Popiah basah (fresh spring rolls) 31
Popiah goreng (deep-fried spring rolls) 32
Potato wedges 121-122

Ramly burger 6, 10, 66-67
Rose syrup 135, 149
Roti canai 38, 41, 43, 85

Sago pearls 145
Sambal belacan 20-22, 87, 106, 110, 113
Sambal sotong kering (cuttlefish sambal) 25, 72
Sambal tumis (fried chilli paste) 20, 25, 47, 75, 78
Satay sauce 63-64
Shallot oil 24, 47, 93, 139
Shallot/onion paste 24, 55, 80-81, 83-86, 94, 101-102
Sotong kangkung 60-61
Soy milk 126-127
Spicy garlic sauce 65
Street food 5-6, 9-10, 17, 26, 29, 37, 47, 62, 91, 139
Sweet sour sauce 53, 64

Tamarind 12, 20, 51, 61, 63, 71, 80, 86-87, 94, 101-102
Tau foo fah (soy milk pudding) 126-127
Tauchu paste 31
Teh tarik 133
Tepung beras pulut (glutinous rice flour) 18, 59, 139
Tofu 15, 17, 37, 51, 101-102, 117, 127
Tofu fried puff 15
Tomato sauce 121-122

Udang kering (dried shrimp) 17, 77

Wantan dumplings 62, 92-93
Wantan mee 6, 22-23, 26, 92-93

Yam/taro 18, 56, 117, 145

ABOUT THE AUTHOR

"She grew up learning how to cook and appreciate traditional dishes from the matriarchs of her family."

Home cook, cookbook collector, and now author, Dayana Wong is a woman of style, with a passion for cultural heritage. It has been her dream to write a beautiful cookbook since she was a child. Her love of food and culture was ingrained in her from young by her Malay mother and Chinese father. She grew up learning how to cook and appreciate traditional dishes from the matriarchs of her family; her fondest memories as a young girl revolve around cooking and sharing meals with loved ones.

In this book, she shares personal childhood memories of growing up on a little island – Penang in Malaysia – and offers tried-and-tested recipes of famous street food from her hometown in an approachable way. Dayana has gathered over 50 recipes of local favourites and added little personal touches that she now, wants to share with you.